home decorating workbooks

candles

candles

Paula Pryke

photography by **James Merrell**

Watson-Guptill Publications / New York

First published in Great Britain in 1998 by
Ryland Peters & Small, Cavendish House,
51–55 Mortimer Street, London W1N 7TD

First published in the United States in 1998 by
Watson-Guptill Publications,
a division of BPI Communications, Inc.,
1515 Broadway, New York, NY 10036

Produced by Sun Fung Offset Binding Co., Ltd
Printed in China

ISBN 0-8230-0552-6

A CIP catalog record for this book is available
from the Library of Congress.

First printing, 1998
1 2 3 4 5 6 7 8 / 05 04 03 02 01 00 99 98

Creative Director **Jacqui Small**

Publishing Director **Anne Ryland**

Designer **Sally Powell**

Editor **Zia Mattocks**

Art Assistant **Sailesh Patel**

Editorial Assistant **Maddalena Bastianelli**

Production **Meryl Silbert**

Illustrator **Lizzie Sanders**

Stylists **Martin Bourne**

Margaret Caselton

Nato Welton

contents

Candlelight is magical and sensuous, and my earliest memories of candlelight are all associated with joyful times, with ritual and celebration—the array of brightly colored candles on top of a favorite birthday cake; the glowing candlelight at Christmas as carols were sung around the tree, or the soft, flickering light from a stunning candelabra at a celebration meal. Even short power outages had a magic of their own, as television was replaced by conversation and the house came alive with the warm glow of simple, utilitarian candlelight. Because of such happy associations, candles—the main light source for hundreds of years—are still widely used, on their own or incorporated into decorations, on special occasions to add a note of festivity, or simply to enhance the workaday atmosphere.

The name comes from the Latin *candere*, which means to be white or to glitter, hence giving light in darkness; and long before Christianity, the flame came to symbolize hope, faith, eternity, and the home. The first candles as we know them— made from papyrus wicks dipped into molten wax or tallow, the traditional dipping method still practiced today—were used by the Romans to light their magnificent banquets and to adorn the altars dedicated to the gods. In the Middle Ages, bees were believed to be messengers from paradise and were so highly esteemed that they could be used as a means of payment. Beeswax candles were greatly prized, and they are still the most expensive candles, valued for their bright light and delicate fragrance. During the medieval period, monasteries saved cooking fat to make candles for everyday use and kept beehives to produce honeycombs for altar candles. Only the wealthy could afford bleached beeswax candles; ordinary folk used tallow candles made from animal fat, which produced black smoke and an offensive smell. Those less fortunate made do with rush lights, fashioned by dipping

thin, hollow reeds, which acted as wicks, into molten wax. For years candles remained an expensive necessity, and all except very poor households still made their own from tallow, usually following the butchering of an animal for winter. One night, Oliver Cromwell (1599–1658) is reported to have found his wife sewing by the light of two candles and, horrified by her extravagance, promptly blew one out.

The quality of candles gradually improved, first with the discovery of spermaceti in the late 18th century, and then with the isolation of stearin from tallow in c. 1823. Both of these substances produced harder candles that dripped less and burned for longer with less smoke and smell. However, it was still not until the second half of the 19th century that affordable store-bought candles could be obtained, and this was mainly due to the widespread use of paraffin wax derived from petroleum. Colorless, odorless paraffin burned more brightly than tallow and was easy to manufacture and release from molds. It spurred the growth of the industry so almost all families could afford to buy candles, which remained the main source of light until the 1920s, when oil lamps and, eventually, electricity took over.

Nowadays candles can be enjoyed as luxury items, to create a sense of magic in the home or simply for pure indulgence—a relaxing bath taken in the romantic light of a scented candle is surely one of the most soothing ways to end a busy day, and a shared meal in the flattering glow of a cluster of flickering votives makes the most ordinary evening a memorable event. There are a million and one creative ways to incorporate candles into the home for all occasions, and the following designs make use of a wide variety of living, dried, scented, and colorful materials, in all kinds of containers and holders, to capture the imagination and inspire creativity. The techniques illustrated will provide all the know-how you need to discover the magic of candles and fill your home with mesmerizing light.

Paula Pryke

far left Old kitchen glasses or jelly jars can be given a new lease on life by gluing cinnamon sticks vertically around their sides to make rustic-looking holders for pillar candles (see pages 16–19).
far left Old kitchen glasses or jelly jars can be given a new lease on life by gluing cinnamon sticks vertically around their sides to make rustic-looking holders for pillar candles (*see* pages 16–19).
left above An iron wall hanging with candle holders in the shape of sculptural twigs was decorated with gardenia leaves and scented votives, held in place with pieces of removable adhesive.
left below For a summery look, fresh kumquats were threaded onto lengths of heavy-gauge wire, which were bent into shape and attached to the chandelier as a foil to the vibrant lime-green candles.
below Colorful candles can be incorporated into plants by taping U-shaped wires to their bases and inserting them into the soil.

room decorations

Chiaroscuro is how artists describe the use of light and shade, and in interiors candles can be used to create wonderful lighting effects. Nowadays, instead of needing candles as a main source of light, we have the luxury of choosing them for esthetic reasons, to enhance our rooms and to create atmosphere and character. In the living and eating areas or the bedroom and bathroom, there are innumerable ways to incorporate candles into the home.

above An old wooden fruit crate has been dressed up with a piece of gold cloth and filled with gravel to make an unusual base for a molded, cactus-shaped candle and the aloe plants surrounding it.
above right Brightly colored everlasting flowers make cheerful decorations, arranged simply around a candle anchored in a pot filled with floral foam.
right Strings of garlic and onions are traditional kitchen decorations, and these have been tied together with raffia and anchored around a beeswax candle using skewers.

top left A simple marguerite daisy has been transformed by carefully placing three candles in florist's candle holders into the soil.

top right Often candles look most effective in groups. These bold vases have been filled with wet floral foam into which has been inserted a single stem of papyrus grass and a beeswax candle taped onto wooden sticks.

above left A shallow dish of glass chips makes a stylish base for these unusual candles.

above right An iron chandelier designed to hold flowerpots looks magical filled with daisies, outdoors or in a conservatory.

right Glass holders for votives can be transformed for a special occasion by decorating them with lengths of colorful ribbon.

trough of flowers

Groups of candles look very effective in long arrangements, and
the flowers have also been grouped to give a greater visual impact
to this formal display. The bold oranges and reds of the trough,
candles, photinia, roses, and pincushion proteas, set against the
lush green leaves, contrast with the rich purple of the delicate
violets to create a strong design that is perfect for making a
dramatic color statement in a predominantly neutral interior.

materials & equipment

terracotta trough, 16½ x 8 x 4¾ inches

1 block floral foam, 21½ x 12½ x 9 inches

1¼-inch chicken wire, 20 x 11 inches

9 orange candles, 10 inches long x ⅞-inch diameter

9 wooden skewers, 4 inches long

24 galax leaves (*Galax*)

8 sprigs photinia (*Photinia*), approximately 6 inches long

12 sprigs lady's mantle (*Alchemilla mollis*), approximately 6 inches long

12 sprigs hebe (*Hebe*) or boxwood (*Buxus*), approximately 6 inches long

15 pincushion proteas (*Leucospermum cordifolium*)

15 orange 'Miracle' roses (*Rosa* 'Miracle')

10 bunches purple violets (*Viola odorata*), 20 stems per bunch

knife • floral tape • floral scissors

medium-gauge floral wire • wire cutters

instructions under flap ➤

nightlights

Nightlights are simple to make using old kitchen glasses for the
candle holders with a selection of leaves and reeds to decorate
them. Nonperishables like preserved leaves and cinnamon are best
for permanent decorations, although fresh leaves and reeds will
last fairly well in a cool room and can easily be replaced when they
dry out. For variation, hollowed-out vegetables or fruits, such as
peppers, artichokes, or apples, also make unusual candle holders.

materials & equipment

globe artichoke (*Cynara* Scolymus Group) • candle, 3¾ inches long x 2½-inch diameter

large variegated aspidistra leaf (*Aspidistra*) • candle, 6 inches long x 2-inch diameter
small bunch bear grass (*Dasylirion*)

for the leaf- and reed-covered nightlights: 5 glasses, 3½ inches high x 3-inch
diameter • 5 candles, 3¾ inches long x 2½-inch diameter

10 laurel leaves (*Laurus nobilis*) • 3 lengths natural raffia, 26 inches long

10 preserved magnolia leaves (*Magnolia*) • gold cord, 26 inches long ·

20 stems snake grass (*Equisetum*), for 34 lengths of 4 inches • bronze rope, 30 inches long

20 stems bamboo (*Arundinaria*), for 34 lengths of 4 inches • red rope, 30 inches long

22 cinnamon sticks (*Cinnamomum camphora*), 5 inches long
plaited natural rope, 30 inches long

knife • floral scissors • double-sided tape • floral glue

instructions under flap ➤

1 Cut the block of floral foam so it will sit in the trough and protrude about ¾ inch above the rim. Soak the floral foam in water until it sinks, which indicates it is fully saturated, then place it in the trough.

2 Cover the top surface of the floral foam with chicken wire, tucking the edges down the sides of the container.

3 Group the candles into three groups of three. Then use a sharp knife to cut about ¾ inch off the base of six of the candles so that the central trio will be taller than the ones on each side of it. Tape the groups of candles together, incorporating three skewers around the base of each trio so the skewers extend about 2½ inches below the candles.

4 Position the candles in a line through the center of the floral foam, with the tall trio of candles in the center and the others an equal distance on each side of it.

5 Start by adding eight of the galax leaves along each long edge and four along each short edge of the floral foam, so the leaves conceal the rim of the container and soften the edges of the arrangement.

6 Next, cut the photinia, lady's mantle, and hebe or boxwood into sprigs approximately 6 inches long. Distribute the stems evenly over the floral foam, using the foliage to create a good overall shape for the arrangement.

7 When you are happy with the basic shape of the display, begin introducing the strong color groups by adding the sturdy-stemmed pincushion proteas in five groups of three and then the orange roses in three groups of five.

8 Wire the bunches of violets with double-leg mounts to reinforce their weak stems. Cut an 8-inch length of wire and bend it into a hairpin shape, making one leg longer than the other. Hold the U-end against the stems and, taking care not to damage the flowers, wind the long leg around the stems and the other leg of wire; then add the violets to the display.

leaf- and reed-covered nightlights

1 The leaves should be fairly uniform in size and long enough to cover the glasses vertically and protrude over the rims. Trim off the stalks to make a straight edge that will align with the base of the glass.

2 Apply glue to the backs of the laurel leaves and position them around one of the glasses, overlapping each leaf almost to the spine of the one adjacent to it. Then cover another glass with the preserved magnolia leaves in the same way.

3 For the three reed-covered nightlights, cut approximately 34 pieces of snake grass and bamboo, roughly 4 inches long, then trim about 22 cinnamon sticks into lengths of 5 inches.

4 Glue the pieces of snake grass, bamboo, and cinnamon vertically around the glasses, making sure they butt up to each other and that the ends are even with the bases of the glasses.

5 Place candles in the glasses. Then wrap the lengths of red rope, bronze rope, and plaited rope twice around the nightlights covered with bamboo, snake grass, and cinnamon respectively; tie neat double knots and trim off the ends.

6 Wrap the length of gold cord twice around the nightlight covered with preserved magnolia leaves, tie a double knot, and trim the ends. Gather the three pieces of raffia together and wrap them twice around the nightlight covered with laurel leaves, tie a neat double knot, and trim off the ends.

artichoke candle holder

1 Using a sharp knife, chop the stalk off a medium-sized artichoke so it will sit flat on the surface.

2 Then, being careful not to damage any of the leaves, cut and scoop out the center of the artichoke.

3 Insert a candle firmly into the hollow space, placing it centrally so it will stand upright without toppling over.

leaf-wrapped candle

1 Cut the stalk off a large variegated aspidistra leaf. Then apply a piece of double-sided tape to the cut edge of the leaf and secure it to the side of the candle, making sure the bottom edge of the leaf is flush with the base of the candle.

2 Carefully wrap the leaf around the candle, overlapping the edges as you work. Use another piece of tape to hold the tip of the leaf in place.

3 Wrap a small bunch of bear grass around the candle and secure it with a double knot. Then trim the ends to about ¾ inch.

rope-wrapped pot of seashells

With a nautical theme that conjures up images of the beach, this simple decoration is perfect for a bathroom and would also make an excellent gift, since the natural hues will blend with any color scheme. When the candle burns down, it can easily be replaced with a new one by carefully removing the shells glued around its base.

materials & equipment

flowerpot, 4 inches high x 5½-inch diameter

approximately 3 yards rope, ½-inch diameter

1 block floral foam, 9 x 4½ x 3 inches

beeswax candle, 5½ inches long x 1¾-inch diameter

4 wooden skewers, 3 inches long

selection of large and small seashells

hot glue gun and glue sticks

knife • tape • scrap paper

instructions under flap ➤

6 It is advisable to use a hot glue gun to apply this decoration, since you will need a fairly large quantity of glue to hold the shells securely in place. Cover your work surface with scrap paper and take care not to let the hot glue drip. Begin gluing the shells around the rim of the flowerpot, evenly distributing the larger shells and using the smaller shells to fill the gaps in between.

7 Work your way around the pot, gradually covering up all the floral foam as you build up the arrangement, moving in toward the base of the candle. Take care to juxtapose shells with a good variation of size, shape, and color.

8 When you have used up all the large shells, use the remaining small shells to fill in any gaps and to alter the shape and balance of the arrangement as necessary.

1 To cover the flowerpot in neat coils of thick natural rope, first apply glue all around the bottom edge of the pot.

2 Position the rope flush around the base of the flowerpot and hold it firmly until the glue has dried. Then wind the rope tightly around the pot, pushing the coils down so the pot is completely hidden. Apply glue around the rim of the pot and glue the last row of rope flush with the top edge of the pot, holding it firmly until the glue has dried.

3 Cut and glue the block of floral foam as necessary so it will sit snugly inside the flowerpot and emerge approximately 1 inch above the rim.

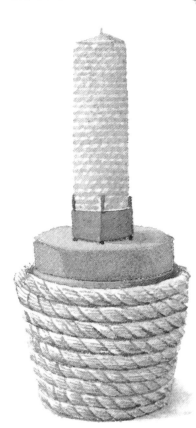

4 Tape four skewers at regular intervals around the base of the candle so they protrude below the base by 1¾ inches.

5 Place the candle in the center of the floral foam.

driftwood sconce

Old pieces of driftwood have been screwed together and two flat stones glued in place to act as candle holders, producing this contemporary-looking wall sconce. The driftwood, with its irregular grain and knots, is the perfect way to introduce natural texture into an interior, and the gray sheen of the wood provides a neutral ground against which to make a dramatic statement with the bold purple candles, chosen to complement the color of the cardoons.

materials & equipment

2 pieces driftwood, 28 x 4 x 1¹/₄ inches and 8¹/₂ x 2¹/₂ x 1¹/₄ inches

2 driftwood sticks, approximately 18 inches and 20 inches long x 1¹/₄-inch diameter

¹/₄ yard rope, ¹/₄-inch diameter

2 flat stones, approximately 3 inches long

2 purple candles, 6¹/₂ inches long x 2-inch diameter

4 stems cardoons (*Cynara cardunculus*)

1 yard rope, ⁷/₈-inch diameter

C-clamp • drill and bit • 6 long wood screws • screwdriver

coarse sandpaper • tape

vise • glue • 2 small nails • hammer

floral scissors • string

instructions under flap ➤

6 Make the hanger for the sconce by clamping the top end of the cross in a vise and drilling two holes 1¼ inches deep vertically through the top edge.

7 Apply glue to the ends of the ¼-inch rope and insert them into the holes, then secure the ends further with two nails tapped in from the front.

8 Glue the two stones onto the flattened ends of the driftwood sticks, then glue a candle to the top of each stone.

9 Arrange the cardoons on the sconce so the flower heads are staggered along its length. Then tie the stems tightly to the driftwood sticks with string.

10 Tie the thick rope twice around the cross, on top of the string, secure it with a double knot, and trim the ends. Hang the sconce from a sturdy nail.

1 Place the short piece of wood on top of the long piece, just below one-third of the way down, to form the arms of the cross. Using a C-clamp, clamp the wood firmly into position.

2 Turn the cross over and drill two holes through the long piece of wood and to a depth of about $1/2$ inch into the short piece. Screw the arms of the cross firmly in place.

3 Use coarse sandpaper to smooth the top of each of the two driftwood sticks to form a flat surface.

4 With the flattened ends of the driftwood sticks at the top, work out where they will best lie vertically along the front of the cross, then tape or clamp the sticks securely into position.

5 To secure the driftwood sticks, turn the cross over and drill two holes near the bottom of the cross, through the back of the shaft and to a depth of $1/2$ inch into the bottom of each of the driftwood sticks. Drill another hole through each arm of the cross and into the top ends of the sticks. Screw the sticks into place.

nut chandelier

This is an ideal, semipermanent decoration for a country-style kitchen or a sunroom. The mixture of smooth- and rough-shelled nuts are a great way to introduce natural colors and textures, and the coarse string from which the candelabra is suspended complements them perfectly. Nuts are often used to make rustic-looking wreaths to hang on walls or doors, and this candelabra is an unusual variation on that traditional idea.

materials & equipment

circular Styrofoam™ wreath frame, 12-inch diameter, 2½ inches wide

4 floral candle holders, 1¼-inch diameter

9 yards natural string, ⅛-inch diameter

2 strips burlap, approximately 8 x 36 inches

5–7 pounds assorted mixed nuts

4 candles, 7 inches long x 1¼-inch diameter

scissors • glue • spool wire • wire cutters

hot glue gun and glue sticks • scrap paper

instructions under flap ➤

6 When the ring is covered, glue the end of the burlap in place. Then, for extra security, bind the burlap-covered ring with spool wire. Twist the ends of the wire tightly together and then push the cut ends back into the wreath frame to conceal them.

7 Place the ring on scrap paper and use a hot glue gun to glue the nuts onto the top and sides of the burlap, grouping them in like clusters and concealing the sides of the candle holders. Then leave the glue to dry.

8 Turn the ring over and glue nuts onto the underside in the same way until the burlap is covered. Leave the glue to dry before turning the ring right side up.

9 Make sure the ring will hang straight, then join the braided ropes with a secure overhand knot. For extra safety, apply glue to the knot, then place the candles in the holders.

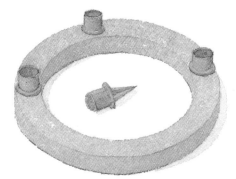

1 Push the candle holders into the Styrofoam™ ring, spacing them at regular intervals apart.

2 Cut the string into three lengths of 1 yard and three of 2 yards. Fold the three longer pieces in half and space them evenly around the ring. Attach them by passing the folded end under the ring, threading the cut ends through the loop and pulling them tight.

3 Take the shorter lengths of string and push one end through the loop in between the other two pieces of string. Apply glue to hold the third piece of string in place and leave it to dry.

4 Plait each group of string, making an overhand knot in the end of each braid to prevent it from unraveling.

5 Glue one end of a burlap strip to the Styrofoam™ ring and wrap it tightly around the ring, pulling the edges up around the candle holders to conceal the plastic. Glue the end of the strip to the ring, then repeat with the second strip of burlap.

right Molded candles come in a bewildering array of shapes, and this sophisticated swirl candle looks stunning in an Art Deco-style holder, which complements its design. The delicate skeletonized leaves around the candle and the collection of shells scattered at its base add the finishing touches.

far right Some cactus growers glue colorful dried flowers onto tiny cacti to give the impression they are flowering naturally. These, displayed with votives in similar holders, make fun table decorations.

top left The straight anthurium stems, cut and packed in small vials of water that are hidden beneath the succulent plants, are able to drink when they are lying horizontally on the shallow glass dish, which makes an excellent modern container.

above left Thin tapers are slender enough to be pushed directly into the soil in between the mixed succulents, planted in a shallow wooden trough, without the need for wires to anchor them in place.

above center These individual posies of starflowers, globeflowers, bluebells, feverfew, and dwarf daffodils, surrounded with ivy leaves and tied with raffia, were supported around the candle with their stems resting in the water by a grid made of thin floral tape.

above right Tall flowers, like irises, can be arranged in the base of a shallow dish by means of a florist's frog (pin holder), popular in Japanese floral design. The frog is attached to the dish with floral adhesive and the ends of the stems are pressed onto the spikes.

right A contemporary combination design—a vase that cleverly up-ends to form a votive holder.

centerpieces & tabletop decorations

No longer a necessity, candlelight is inextricably associated with romance and has a
soothing, calming effect that creates the perfect atmosphere for entertaining. Whether
the occasion is an intimate meal for two or a larger affair to mark a special occasion,
candlelight is a must—and the soft, warm glow is the most forgiving and flattering light.
There is such a wide variety of candles and holders available that the possibilities for
creating unusual table settings are endless, from simple, chic ideas to tie in with the color
scheme of your room or table linen to more elaborate themed displays for celebrations.

left I am a huge fan of displays
of a single flower type, and English
ranunculi are my favorite. These
are shown in a votive holder that
was specially designed in France.
below left Some of the most
effective decorations are bowls
of inexpensive floating candles.
These silver candles float in a
stylish glass bowl on a pile of silver
stones for a contemporary look.
bottom left An oversized glass
makes an elegant centerpiece for
a dinner party, and the swirl of
bear grass adds a natural touch
to a lotus-flower candle.
below Trailing ivy with crab
apples, lotus flowers, and beeswax
candles in colorful pots make a
cheerful low-cost table decoration.

candelabra with velvet & grapes

A standard metal candelabra has been completely transformed into a stunning centerpiece for a special occasion by wrapping the stand in green velvet ribbon and adorning it with bunches of grapes. The natural beeswax candles and the predominance of white grapes accentuate the fresh, summery look of the display.

materials & equipment

metal candelabra with 4 arms and 3 feet, 24 inches high

11 yards dark green velvet ribbon, 1¼ inches wide

approximately 5 pounds red and white grapes (*Vitis vinifera*)

4 beeswax candles, 10 inches long x ⅝-inch diameter

double-sided tape • floral scissors

spool wire • wire cutters

instructions under flap ➤

5 Attach the end of the ribbon to the end of the final arm and wind the ribbon neatly around the central column, down the last central spoke, and to the end of the third foot, securing the end as before.

6 First divide the grapes into roughly equal bunches. Arrange one bunch around one of the candle holders, then, using spool wire, bind its stalk to the candelabra. In the same way, bind the stalk of another bunch to the arm of the candelabra so the grapes hang down from the arm.

7 Attach three more bunches so they lie around the other candle holders. Then hang the remaining bunches from the arms and the central spokes, and lay some around the feet, distributing the colors evenly.

1 Starting at the end of one arm of the candelabra, attach the underside of the ribbon to the metal with a piece of double-sided tape. Wind the ribbon tightly around the metal arm, overlapping each turn by at least $1/2$ inch. Neatly encircle the base of the candle holder and continue winding the ribbon around the arm.

2 Where the arm joins the central column, take the ribbon across to the adjacent arm and wind it around the second arm, securing the end with double-sided tape.

3 Attach the ribbon to the top of the central column. Wind it down one of the central spokes and continue to the end of one of the feet.

4 Start at the end of one of the feet and wind the ribbon up to the point where the arms meet; cut the ribbon and secure the end with tape.

hurricane lamp with everlasting roses

Freeze-dried roses look so natural that they can easily fool people into believing they are fresh, making them an excellent choice for a long-lasting table decoration. The hurricane lamp makes this arrangement perfect for outdoors, since it protects the flame from breezes and prevents the wax from dripping onto the flowers.

materials & equipment

Styrofoam™ hurricane-lamp base, approximately 8½-inch diameter, or 2 blocks floral foam, 9 x 4½ x 3 inches

glass hurricane lamp, preferably with glass base

3 bunches preserved galax leaves (*Galax*)

12 pink and 12 red freeze-dried roses (*Rosa*)

15 pink cockscomb (*Celosia argentea*)

2 bunches marjoram (*Origanum*)

pink candle, 6 inches long x 1¼-inch diameter

floral glue • 2 pencils • string • knife

fine- and medium-gauge floral wire • wire cutters • floral scissors

instructions under flap ➤

7 To wire each rose with a double-leg mount, bend a piece of medium-gauge wire, 8 inches long, into a hairpin shape, with one leg longer than the other. Hold the U-end against the top of the rose's stem and wind the long leg around the stem and the other leg of wire. Then add the wired roses, alternating the colors and the angle of each one to create a rounded display.

8 Wire the cockscomb and sprigs of marjoram in the same way, and use them to fill in the gaps between the roses.

9 Cut the stalks off the five unwired galax leaves so the hurricane lamp will sit flat on top of them. Then glue or pin them to the base to conceal the floral foam.

10 Finally, place the hurricane lamp in the center of the arrangement and place the candle inside. It is best to use a hurricane lamp with a glass base so the wax will be retained in the bottom; this will prevent any damage to the arrangement and protect the dried flowers from the heat.

1 If you are unable to purchase a Styrofoam™ hurricane-lamp base, glue together the long sides of two blocks of floral foam. Then draw a circle with a diameter of about 8½ inches. If you do not have a suitable circular shape to draw around, tie two pencils 4½ inches apart with a length of string and use them as a compass, holding one stationary in the center of the block and drawing a circle around it with the other.

2 With the pencil line as your guide, use a sharp knife to cut the floral foam block into a circle.

3 Place the glass hurricane lamp in the center of the foam circle and draw around the base with a pencil.

4 Carve away the sharp edge of the foam circle, holding the knife at an angle so the surface will curve gently away from the base of the hurricane lamp.

5 Set aside five of the galax leaves; then, using pieces of fine-gauge wire 8 inches long, wire up the others by threading a wire through the spine, bringing the two ends together, and twisting them around the stem to make a double-leg mount.

6 Leaving the central area clear for the hurricane lamp, place the wired galax leaves evenly over the floral foam.

fall berries

There is no better time than the fall to make the most of the diversity of foliage, with the wonderful shades of the leaves as they turn and the abundance of berries that are often left on bushes that have lost their leaves. Long, low arrangements are ideal for rectangular tables, and there are so many different colors and textures that, following this basic method, you can easily make substitutions to create a pleasing display at any time of year.

materials & equipment

green plastic tray, 19½ x 4⅞ x 1¼ inches

2 blocks floral foam, 9 x 4½ x 3 inches

orange candle, 12 inches long x 3-inch diameter

4 wooden garden stakes, 5 inches long

16 strands trailing ivy (*Hedera*), 14–22 inches long

22 sprigs guelder rose (*Viburnum opulus*), 6–10 inches long

5 ornamental cabbages (*Brassica*)

20 sprigs rosehips (*Rosa*), 6–10 inches long

8 sprigs photinia (*Photinia*), 10 inches long

15 sprigs smoke bush (*Cotinus*), approximately 8 inches long

12 sprigs variegated mint (*Mentha*), approximately 10 inches long

4 oak leaves (*Quercus*), approximately 10 inches long

12 sprigs variegated pittosporum (*Pittosporum*), 8–10 inches long

knife • floral tape • floral scissors

instructions under flap ➤

6 Remove any unattractive outer leaves from the five ornamental cabbages, then add them to the display, staggering them along the length of the arrangement.

7 Evenly distribute the sprigs of rosehips over the arrangement. Then add all the remaining foliage, apart from the variegated pittosporum, spacing the colors evenly over the decoration and taking care to conceal all the floral foam.

8 Fill in any gaps with the variegated pittosporum. Make sure you are happy with the color balance, then trim any straggling pieces of ivy to tidy up the arrangement.

1 Trim the blocks of floral foam as necessary to fit them into the tray. Thoroughly soak the foam in water, then replace the blocks in the tray and wind floral tape securely around them to hold them in place.

2 Tape the garden stakes around the base of the candle so they protrude about 3½ inches below the base.

3 Push the stakes into the the floral foam to anchor the candle in place in the center of the arrangement.

4 Arrange the strands of ivy evenly over the floral foam so they conceal the edges of the tray, with the longer strands lying out from the center toward the short sides of the display, and the shorter strands lying outward along the length of the arrangement.

5 Strip the lower leaves off the sprigs of guelder rose, then distribute them evenly over the floral foam.

wrapped vases

A simple vase can be dressed up to stunning effect with any piece of fabric, whether opulent velvet, textured silk, or checked cotton. These two examples create very different looks: the rich burgundy velvet is set off by the gold and bronze decorations, creating an elegant display for a winter dinner party; the same vase wrapped in cerise silk, with a beeswax candle, fresh berries, and brightly colored roses, is pretty and cheerful for an informal supper.

materials & equipment

glass vase with lip, 7 inches high x 6-inch diameter at mouth

dark red velvet, 24 x 24 inches

1 yard antique gold rope, ¼-inch diameter

ribbed candle, 10 inches long x 3-inch diameter

9 wooden skewers, 5 inches long

4 sprigs fruiting ivy (*Hedera*), approximately 6 inches long

5 small decorative pine cones

copper spray paint

antique gold spray paint

tape • scrap paper • floral glue

 instructions under flap ➤

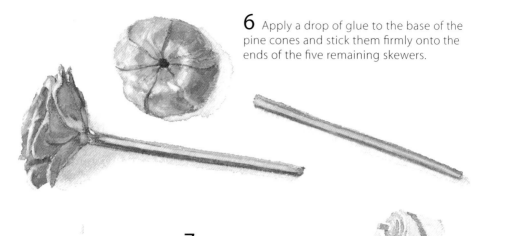

6 Apply a drop of glue to the base of the pine cones and stick them firmly onto the ends of the five remaining skewers.

7 Lay the pine cones on a sheet of scrap paper and spray them thoroughly with antique gold paint, then leave them to dry.

8 Arrange the sprigs of fruiting ivy and the pine cones around the candle, tucking them into the mouth of the vase.

for the summer version:

1 Wrap the vase in cerise shot-silk fabric and tie a length of silver rope around the neck of the vase. Then add a natural beeswax candle, taped onto wooden skewers as before.

2 Use natural sprigs of fruiting ivy and a selection of brightly colored fresh roses in orange, yellow, lilac, and pink to arrange around the candle.

1 Lay the fabric right side down on the work surface and stand the vase in the center of the square. Bring one of the corners up and tuck the fabric neatly inside the vase.

2 Work your way around the vase, bringing the fabric up and tucking it into the mouth of the vase until it is entirely covered.

3 Alter the folds of the fabric to make them even, then wrap the length of gold rope twice around the fabric just beneath the rim of the vase and secure it with a neat double knot.

4 Tape four skewers at evenly spaced intervals around the base of the candle so they will rest on the bottom of the vase and support the candle at the correct height. Place the candle in the vase.

5 Lay out the sprigs of fruiting ivy on a sheet of scrap paper and spray them thoroughly with copper paint, then leave them to dry.

opposite
Oranges, lemons, and cut limes float among the scented candles in this plain glass bowl to produce a fresh, tangy fragrance. The addition of the Chinese lanterns and sunflower heads enhances this vibrant decoration.

above Arrangements of floating flower heads were popular in the 1920s and 1930s, when blooms were typically scattered around a bird figurine. In this romantic display, the scented candles and gloriously perfumed gardenia flowers float around a candlestick that has been placed in the center of the bowl. The great thing about a simple decoration like this one is that once you have settled on your bowl and candles, it is easy and inexpensive to assemble.

above right This tall candelabra incorporates an openwork metal bowl designed to hold flower arrangements. The bowl has been lined with large aspidistra leaves and filled with wet floral foam, which is covered with a wonderful cascade of foliage and white perfumed flowers, including eucalyptus, lilac, and lilies.

right Another clever design is this combined candelabra and vase, which contains a lovely summery mix of lilac hydrangeas, blue delphiniums, and pink roses. These 'Mainzer Fastnach' roses are one of my favorite scented flowers and look especially pretty alongside the blousy hydrangeas, both of which are offset perfectly by the spiky aromatic rosemary.

scented displays
The beneficial properties of essential oils and the powers of fragrances to stimulate or relax the mind and evoke memories are proven, and the wonderful combination of scent and candlelight creates the perfect atmosphere in which to unwind after a long day. Since so many fragrances are plant-derived, it is most fitting to use natural aromatic materials, such as fruits or spices, with scented or natural beeswax candles. Favorite scented flowers include honeysuckle, lavender, jasmine, and roses, but there are myriad other fruits and herbs in the garden with lovely perfumes.

far left Most fresh herbs are wonderfully aromatic, and a selection specially chosen to include a wide range of foliage, from dark green spikes of chives to the delicate fronds of fennel, can make an unusual alternative to cut flowers. These colorful frosted glasses are perfect containers for bunches of fresh chives, mint, fennel, sage, thyme, parsley, and cilantro. The brightly colored tapers, which are wired with double-leg mounts that rest on the bases of the cups, transform them into a cheerful decoration for a kitchen table or windowsill.
left Cloves were mixed into the molten wax to give these candles a warm, spicy scent as they burn.

rosemary & roses

Many flowers have a lovely scent, and this arrangement has a few of the best. The fragrance of paper whites is wonderfully heady, and the 'Jacaranda' roses are one of the few scented varieties of roses that are available all year round. In the past, growers deliberately bred the perfume out of flowers because nonscented varieties lasted longer, but nowadays growers are producing hybrids that are both long lasting and scented.

materials & equipment

plastic bowl or flowerpot, 3 inches high x 7-inch diameter

2 blocks floral foam, 9 x 4¹/₂ x 3 inches

50 sprigs rosemary (*Rosmarinus officinalis*), 4¹/₂ inches long

1¹/₈ yards silver rope, ¹/₆-inch diameter

3 lilac beeswax candles, 8 inches long x 1¹/₄-inch diameter

7 sprigs fruiting ivy (*Hedera*)

10 pink 'Jacaranda' roses (*Rosa* 'Jacaranda')

15 lilac 'Delilah' roses (*R.* 'Delilah')

6 purple calla lilies (*Zantedeschia*)

15 paper whites (*Narcissus papyraceus*)

knife • floral glue • floral scissors • double-sided tape

medium-gauge floral wire • wire cutters • floral tape

instructions under flap ➤

5 Distribute the sprigs of fruiting ivy evenly over the bowl, making use of the berries around the edge of the display to hide the rim of the container and the floral foam. Try to arrange the sprigs over the surface so they create a dome shape.

6 The flowers should be arranged in groups to make a strong visual impact. Start first with the scented pink 'Jacaranda' roses in two groups of five, and then add the lilac 'Delilah' roses in three groups of five.

7 Next, place the purple calla lilies in between the five groups of pink and lilac roses to provide dramatic contrast.

8 Finally, divide the 15 scented paper whites into five groups of three stems. Then add them to the display, making sure you create a good color balance.

1 Cut and glue the floral foam to fit snugly inside the container, resting it on small blocks of spare foam if necessary so it protrudes at least 1¼ inches above the rim of the bowl to create the rounded, domed effect. Thoroughly soak the floral foam in water and then place it in the pot.

2 Cut the rosemary into neat sprigs of approximately 4½ inches, checking that this is long enough to cover the sides of the pot and the floral foam. Place three horizontal rows of double-sided tape around the outside of the bowl and attach the sprigs vertically around the pot until all the plastic is hidden.

3 Wrap the length of silver rope twice around the center of the pot to hold the rosemary in place, and tie a neat double knot.

4 Cut six 3-inch pieces of wire and bend them into hairpin shapes, then tape two of the U-ends onto each side of the base of each candle. Push the wires into the floral foam, placing the candles in a triangular formation.

53

candlestick with foliage & limes

Bushy stems of lush green leaves, such as boxwood or hebe, can be wired onto a standard candlestick to make a natural foliage base. This has been decorated for a wedding with delicate, star-shaped stephanotis, which are short-lived but have a lovely fragrance. In contrast are the sturdy half-limes, which emit a fresh, zesty scent.

materials & equipment

iron candlestick with 4 legs, 27 inches high

approximately 78 sprigs of bushy foliage,
such as boxwood (*Buxus*) or hebe (*Hebe*)

20 stems stephanotis (*Stephanotis floribunda*)

10 limes (*Citrus aurantiifolia*)

beeswax candle, 9 inches long x 3-inch diameter

floral scissors • wire cutters

medium-gauge floral wire • fine-gauge floral wire • knife

instructions under flap ➤

6 Slice the limes in half, then cut 20 pieces of medium-gauge wire, 5 inches long. Push a wire through the back of each half-fruit and twist the two ends together.

7 To fasten the limes around the candlestick, separate the two ends of wire and push them in between the sprigs of foliage, with one wire on each side of the candlestick's metal stem. Twist the wires together tightly against the candlestick so the limes are held securely in place, then snip off the wire ends. The lengths of wire should be completely concealed among the leaves.

8 Add the remaining limes in the same way, spacing them evenly over the stem and legs of the candlestick. Finally, place the candle on the candle holder.

1 Cut approximately 30 sprigs of the boxwood or hebe into lengths of 6 inches to cover the main stem of the candlestick. Then cut approximately 48 sprigs to about 2 inches to cover the feet.

2 Starting at the top of the candlestick, arrange about six sprigs of foliage around the main stem, positioning them so the top leaves are pushed out by the base of the candle holder. Bind the stems in place with a length of medium-gauge wire.

3 Add five more rows of foliage in the same way, working down the candlestick toward the feet. Make sure all the stems point down and the leaves of each new row overlap the stems of the row above to conceal the wire and create the bushy effect. Use 12 of the shorter sprigs to cover each of the feet, binding them onto the frame in three rows of four sprigs.

4 Cut the delicate stephanotis into sprigs of approximately 2³/₄ inches. To wire the stephanotis with double-leg mounts, cut pieces of fine-gauge wire, 4 inches long, and bend them into hairpin shapes, making one leg longer than the other. Hold the U-end against the stem, wind the long leg around the flower stem and the short leg, then bring the two wires together.

5 Add the wired stephanotis to the candlestick, pushing the wire legs down at an angle of about 45° in between the sprigs of foliage so the wires are completely concealed among the leaves.

cone of citrus fruit

Citrus fruit has a wonderful fresh scent that conjures up warm evenings in southern European cities like Seville, where the fragrance of ripe oranges pervades the air. The conical candle crowning the stack of fruit was the inspiration for this unusual display, which builds up with layers of satsumas, lemons, and limes interspersed with glossy leaves and is surrounded by spherical candles that echo the symmetry of the satsumas.

materials & equipment

2 blocks floral foam, 9 x 4½ x 3 inches

circular plastic wreath base filled with floral foam,
12-inch diameter, 2½ inches wide

½-inch plywood, cut into a circle 12 inches in diameter

1¼-inch chicken wire, 12 x 32 inches

6 wooden garden stakes, 13 inches long

approximately 60 sprigs ivy (*Hedera*), 4–8 inches long, and 60 ivy leaves

approximately 25 satsumas (*Citrus unshiu*), 27 limes (*Citrus aurantiifolia*),
and 19 lemons (*Citrus limon*)

conical scented candle, 6½ inches x 3-inch diameter at base

5 spherical candles, approximately 3-inch diameter at widest point

knife • glue • floral scissors • medium-gauge floral wire • wire cutters • skewer

instructions under flap ➤

7 Add the first row of approximately 15 satsumas around the base of the cone, pushing the wires into the sides of the floral foam so the fruits rest on the inner edge of the ring.

8 Add a row of about 17 wired limes above the satsumas, filling the gaps between the rows of fruit with ivy leaves.

9 Build up the rest of the cone design with rows of approximately 13 lemons, 10 satsumas, 10 limes, and, last, 6 lemons, filling the gaps between the rows of fruit with ivy leaves.

10 Using a skewer, make a central hole in the base of the conical candle so it fits onto the garden stake protruding from the cone. Conceal any visible floral foam with a final row of ivy leaves, then surround the finished cone of citrus fruit with the spherical scented candles.

62

1 Cut down the length of one of the blocks of floral foam so it will fit comfortably into the center of the circular wreath base. Apply glue to one end of the other block and place it centrally on top of the first, then leave the glue to dry.

2 Use a sharp knife to trim the blocks of floral foam into a roughly conical shape, leaving a flat area on top about the same diameter as the base of the conical candle. Thoroughly soak the wreath frame and the cone in water.

3 To make the finished arrangement easier to move around and to protect your surface from the wet floral foam, place the wreath base on the circular piece of plywood before placing the cone-shaped block in the center of the circle. Then wrap chicken wire around the cone, cut away the excess wire, and twist the edges together to fasten them.

4 Weave five of the garden stakes from top to bottom through the wire to accentuate the cone shape, pushing the ends of the stakes into the wreath frame. Insert the last stake vertically through the center of the cone so it protrudes from the top by about ¾ inch.

5 Cover the circular wreath with sprigs of ivy, 4–8 inches long, pushing the stems into the floral foam.

6 To wire the fruit, cut 10-inch lengths of wire and push one through each fruit, just below halfway, then twist the ends together. Remember, since the sizes of satsumas, lemons, and limes vary, you may need more or less than the numbers given.

spring & summer celebrations

Many cultures mark important events with flowers, food, and candles, since candlelight instantly enhances the atmosphere and evokes a sense of occasion. In my opinion, no celebration is complete without candles and, as long as your venue is insured for their use, there are no rules as to when you should burn them, whether indoors or out, since even during the summer, daylight can be cloudy and gray. In 1525 the citizens of Paris were ordered to place candle lanterns outside their homes, and these, together with glass votive holders and hurricane lamps, are still a popular, practical way to use candles outdoors.

far left Perfect for an Easter party, these little candles molded in the shape of eggs can be displayed in colorful egg cups or even traditional cardboard egg boxes. The centerpiece is a topiary of blown eggs and straw glued in tiers around a cone of floral foam. *left* Create a beach look for a summer party with these lovely molded starfish candles. The ocean theme is continued by the shells, starfish, and sand—a great nonflammable base for candles.

above These floating candles were surrounded by meadow-style spring flowers—cowslips, grape hyacinths, and thrift—arranged to look as if they are growing over the wet floral foam wreath frame, which sits snugly around the straight-sided bowl. *left* Food dye was added to the water of this display of foxgloves, delphiniums, peonies, bergamot, orache, alliums, and astilbe to create a rich, dramatic effect for a party.

right Fish fanatics will love this unusual glass fish bowl, which has a central column designed to hold a candle. Athough it makes an interesting alternative to an ordinary centerpiece, it should only be used as an occasional home for goldfish.

below These ribbon roses (*see* page 94) have been made in cheerful summery colors to match the vibrant candles and plates. Here, they are wired onto a metal ring, but can be re-used time and again.

above This iron chandelier, complete with glass bowls, can be decorated to stunning effect. The candles were attached to the frame at intervals with lengths of pink raffia wound tightly around them and tied in the front with a bow. The mixed ranunculi were cut to length, and the different-colored flowers were distributed evenly among the bowls.

left Colored lamp oil can be used indoors or out as a clean alternative to candles. Before being filled with red, blue, and indigo lamp oil, these stylish oil holders were anchored in gravel in the base of a galvanized vase. This was filled with water, and then the bold marigolds were added for dramatic contrast.

golden pedestal

Single candles on pedestals are great for flanking an aisle at a wedding, and they make lovely freestanding decorations for a party. Arrangements like this are easy to make by taping a block of floral foam onto the candle holder of a tall candlestick. The choice of poppies as the predominant flowers, together with the trailing foliage in myriad shades of green, prevent the display from looking too formal and are reminiscent of summer meadows.

materials & equipment

gold candlestick, 36 inches high

1 block floral foam, 8 x 4 x 3 inches

2-inch chicken wire, 20 x 20 inches

candle, 14 inches long x 2½-inch diameter

7 strands trailing ivy (*Hedera*), approximately 36 inches long

4 stems Solomon's seal (*Polygonatum*)

10 stems spurge (*Euphorbia myrsinites*)

10 stems hebe (*Hebe*) or boxwood (*Buxus*)

6 stems asparagus fern (*Asparagus densiflorus*)

20 stems lady's mantle (*Alchemilla mollis*)

50 orange, yellow, and cream Iceland poppies (*Papaver*)

floral tape • spool wire • heavy-gauge floral wire • wire cutters • floral scissors

instructions under flap ➤

5 Gather the strands of ivy together at the base of the candlestick and bind them to the metal frame using spool wire.

6 Then, working from the bottom up toward the base of the candle, add the trailing Solomon's seal, spurge, and hebe or boxwood, spacing them evenly over the floral foam.

7 Next add the delicate asparagus fern and the lady's mantle, filling in any gaps to create a good background foliage for the poppies.

8 Poppies have a milky sap and require special conditioning. To keep the sap in the stems and maintain their sturdiness, singe the stem ends over the flame of a candle or match. If you need to cut the stems to suit the shape of the display, reseal the cut ends by singeing them again. Finally, distribute the colored poppies evenly over the arrangement.

1 Soak the floral foam in water and then place the block on its end on the pricket of the candlestick. Tape it securely in place by passing the tape twice over the block and under the candle holder in both directions.

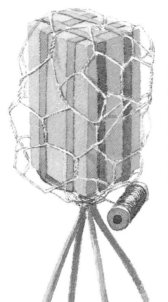

2 Cover the floral foam block with chicken wire and twist the edges tightly together beneath the candle holder. Then wind a length of spool wire around the top of the candlestick to bind the chicken wire in place.

3 Cut three 12-inch lengths of heavy-gauge wire. Bend them into hairpin shapes and tape the U-ends around the base of the candle, approximately 1 inch above its base. Insert the ends of the wire into the floral foam so the candle sits in the center.

4 Push the strands of ivy into the base of the floral foam block, spacing them evenly apart. Leave three of the long strands hanging down loose and twist the other four stems around the legs of the stand.

dais display

Candlelight is always flattering to the face, so here a dais for a wedding or other special function is set with a low, trailing flower arrangement that incorporates three natural beeswax candles of different heights to create visual interest. When arranging flowers like this, it is always a good idea to assemble the display in situ so you can check that it is not too tall and that the hosts and special guests will be clearly visible to the whole party.

materials & equipment

plastic tray, 18½ x 5 x ¾ inches

2 blocks floral foam, 9 x 4½ x 3 inches

3 beeswax candles, 5 inches long x 2½-inch diameter

9 wooden garden stakes, 3 inches long

15 strands trailing ivy (*Hedera*), approximately 20 inches long

5 stems spirea (*Spiraea*), approximately 10 inches long

9 stems asparagus fern (*Asparagus densiflorus*), approximately 20 inches long

8 sprigs spurge (*Euphorbia myrsinites*), 6–8 inches long

4 sprigs dill (*Anethum graveolens*), 6–8 inches long·

8 pink 'Anna' roses (*Rosa* 'Anna') • 20 bright pink 'Ravel' roses (*R.* 'Ravel')
14 peach 'Macarena' roses (*R.* 'Macarena')

7 sprigs guelder rose (*Viburnum opulus*), 6–8 inches long

7 sprigs cockscomb (*Celosia argentea*), 6–8 inches long

10 glory lilies (*Gloriosa*)

floral tape • knife • plastic sheet • floral scissors

instructions under flap ➤

5 Begin filling out the shape of the arrangement with the spurge and dill to create a base of foliage, making sure there is a good variation of color and texture across the display.

6 Next, add the focal flowers—the roses, guelder roses, and cockscomb—taking care to distribute the colors evenly throughout the arrangement.

7 Complete the display by adding the delicate glory lilies, making sure they are distributed evenly among the other flowers to create a good balance.

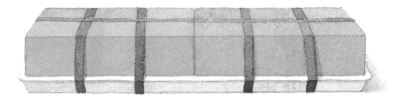

1 Thoroughly soak the blocks of floral foam in water, then place them in the plastic tray and use floral tape to hold them in position.

2 Using a sharp knife, cut between ½ inch and ¾ inch off the bases of two of the candles to make them all different heights, then tape three stakes to the bottom of each.

3 Place the candles in the floral foam, grouping them together in a staggered line across the center of the arrangement.

4 It will be easier to assemble this display in situ, so protect your surface with a plastic sheet. First arrange all the trailing foliage—the ivy, spirea, and asparagus fern—placing it mainly around the edges of the floral foam so the long strands conceal the ridge of the tray.

cherry blossom candelabra

An ordinary candelabra can be transformed into a fairytale display by covering it with a base of sculptural twigs and moss, which can be adorned with cherry blossom in spring and berried twigs in winter. The delicate flowers around the base of the "tree" add to the romance, making a perfect centerpiece for a wedding.

materials & equipment

iron candelabra with solid base, 6 arms, and a central candle holder, 28 inches high

plastic tray, 8½ x 8½ x 1¼ inches

1 block floral foam, 9 x 4½ x 3 inches

3 bunches birch twigs (*Betula*)

carpet moss, approximate total area 10 x 10 inches

approximately 40 sprigs cherry blossom (*Prunus*), 3 inches long

20 stems fritillary (*Fritillaria pinardii*)

7 candles, 7 inches long x 1¼-inch diameter

knife • floral tape • spool wire • wire cutters • floral scissors • floral glue • floral wire

6 Cut the blossoms into small sprigs and space them evenly over the candelabra, pushing their sturdy stems in between the birch twigs. Save a few sprigs of blossom to decorate the base.

7 Place the fritillary flowers around the main stem of the candelabra, pushing the stems through the layer of moss and into the floral foam. Add a few sprigs of cherry blossom to the base of the candelabra in the same way.

8 As the birch twigs increase the size of the candelabra, it will look more balanced with thicker candles than it normally holds, so shave the bases with a knife to fit them into the holders.

9 Glue clumps of moss around the candle holders to conceal the metal and the shaved bases of the candles.

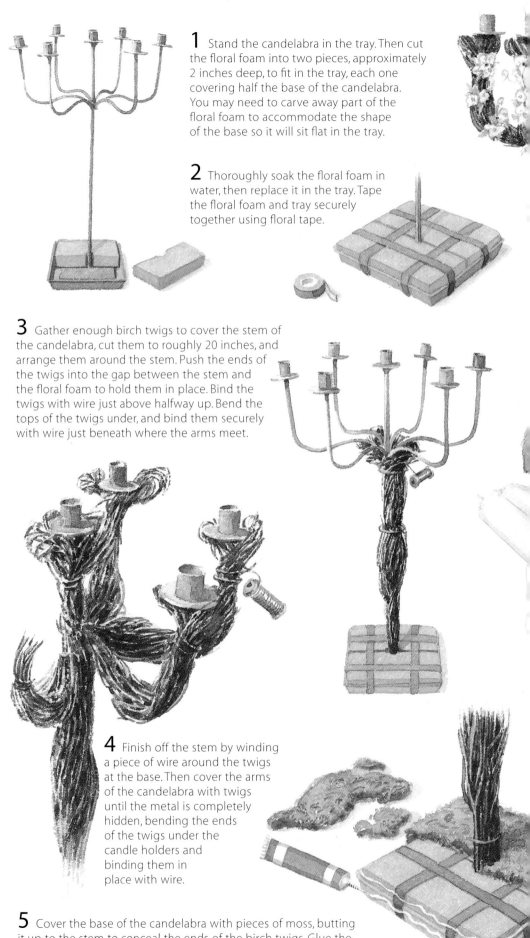

1 Stand the candelabra in the tray. Then cut the floral foam into two pieces, approximately 2 inches deep, to fit in the tray, each one covering half the base of the candelabra. You may need to carve away part of the floral foam to accommodate the shape of the base so it will sit flat in the tray.

2 Thoroughly soak the floral foam in water, then replace it in the tray. Tape the floral foam and tray securely together using floral tape.

3 Gather enough birch twigs to cover the stem of the candelabra, cut them to roughly 20 inches, and arrange them around the stem. Push the ends of the twigs into the gap between the stem and the floral foam to hold them in place. Bind the twigs with wire just above halfway up. Bend the tops of the twigs under, and bind them securely with wire just beneath where the arms meet.

4 Finish off the stem by winding a piece of wire around the twigs at the base. Then cover the arms of the candelabra with twigs until the metal is completely hidden, bending the ends of the twigs under the candle holders and binding them in place with wire.

5 Cover the base of the candelabra with pieces of moss, butting it up to the stem to conceal the ends of the birch twigs. Glue the moss to the sides of the tray and use 2-inch lengths of floral wire bent into hairpin shapes to secure the top area to the wet floral foam.

floral chandelier

I love hanging decorations, and I always recommend them if the occasion is right and there is a strong place from which to hang them. Here, a basic iron candelabra has first had blocks of floral foam taped onto it and then been adorned with fresh flowers to make a summery canopy for guests to admire. The beeswax candles give off a subtle sweet fragrance as they burn, which mingles well with the delicate scent of the flowers.

materials & equipment

iron chandelier with 6 candle holders, 20-inch diameter

6 caged floral foam domes, 4-inch diameter

6 blocks floral foam, 3 x 4½ x 3 inches

6 beeswax candles, 5 inches long x 2½-inch diameter

7 branches lilac (*Syringa*)

7 branches dusty miller (*Senecio cineraria*)

6 sprigs Solomon's seal (*Polygonatum*)

10 sprigs spurge (*Euphorbia myrsinites*)

1 branch cherry blossom (*Prunus*)

10 flag irises (*Iris*)

10 pink hydrangeas (*Hydrangea*)

10 white double lisianthus (*Eustoma grandiflorum*)

heavy-gauge floral wire • wire cutters • knife • floral tape

removable adhesive blocks • floral scissors

instructions under flap ➤

5 Anchor the chandelier at a height where you are able to work on both the top and the underside. Begin adding the flowers to the blocks, starting with the tougher sprigs of lilac and dusty miller: there is very little floral foam in the caged domes, so leave the smaller sprigs for these areas.

6 Next, add the Solomon's seal, spurge, cherry blossom, and irises to create a good base with an even distribution of color. Then add the filler flowers—the large hydrangeas. Take care not to place all the heads at the same height, as this will make the arrangement look heavy. Work around the frame in a zigzag manner, placing some stems higher than others.

7 Carefully add the very delicate double lisianthus, distributing them evenly over the arrangement. Finally, make sure you have covered all the areas of floral foam and that the display is well balanced and hangs straight.

1 Thoroughly soak the floral foam blocks and caged domes in water. Then attach the six domes as follows: thread a 10-inch length of heavy-gauge wire through each of the flat bases and wrap the ends around the frame of the chandelier, positioning one dome centrally between each pair of candle holders. Twist the wires together tightly so the caged floral foam domes are suspended at an angle, facing out and down.

2 Use floral tape to attach the wet blocks of floral foam onto the metal frame in between the candle holders, directly above the caged floral foam domes, cutting the blocks to fit over the metal fastenings that attach the hanging chain to the iron frame.

3 Before you begin arranging the flowers, place the beeswax candles in the holders to give you an idea of the overall height of the design you are creating. If the candle holders do not have prickets, use removable adhesive to secure the candles in place.

4 Cut all the flower and foliage stems to lengths of between 2 inches and 8 inches. Bear in mind that the longer pieces will be used on the underside of the chandelier to create the trailing effect, while the shorter stems will be used to fill in the top area. The sides and underside will be viewed more than the top of the display, so use your best material there.

above Pine cones last indefinitely and are ideal for using in autumnal decorations. These have been left natural and glued over a gilded wire lantern and around the base of a beeswax candle placed inside.

above These small candles are widely available in silver and gold and look lovely grouped together in miniature gilded flowerpots filled with gravel and placed on an occasional table or mantelpiece.

above A cluster of ornamental gourds around a candle is perfect for Halloween. These are coated with yacht varnish to preserve them and anchored into the floral foam with heavy-gauge floral wires.

fall & winter festivals
Candles have been used to illuminate major festivals for hundreds of years, and they remain a simple, inexpensive way to add a note of festivity to most occasions. Candles are often lit at Thanksgiving celebrations; they are placed in carved-out pumpkins on Halloween to make jack-o'-lanterns to ward off evil spirits; and wherever Christmas is observed, candles invariably occupy a place of honor.

above and right Candles can be purchased in all shapes and sizes, especially in the months leading up to Christmas. A few gold candles in the shape of large pebbles can be used to great effect by displaying them alongside a handful of stones that have been sprayed with gold paint. The collection looks stunning placed in a random manner on a low decorative table, such as this gilded mosaic one, and is ideal for a party.

top left A candelabra with dramatic burgundy candles in glass holders has been decorated with sculptural birch twigs, which were spray-painted coppery pink and then sprinkled with silver glitter while the paint was still wet, making a contemporary alternative to a traditional Christmas tree.

top right Ideal for a winter party, these simple votive holders, made from fresh oranges studded with cloves with a hole carved in the top, can be placed anywhere in the home to impart a wonderful spicy scent—on a mantelpiece, table, or windowsill, or tied with gold rope and hung on a Christmas tree.

above With the inclusion of silver candles and seedheads, this seasonal arrangement of fir and berries with wonderfully scented white lilies, roses, and sprigs of rosemary, makes a lovely Christmas centerpiece.

ring of hops

Hops are evocative of the countryside at harvest time, so they are the obvious choice for any arrangement made to celebrate this time of year. This attractive rustic display is surprisingly simple to make—all you need for the basic structure are a sturdy metal ring and four large pillar candles. Natural sisal rope is used to tie the ring to the outside of the candles that support it, providing a frame onto which the fresh hops can be bound with wire.

materials & equipment

4 candles, 8 inches long x 4-inch diameter

1 metal ring wreath frame, 15-inch diameter

6 yards sisal rope, ¹⁄₄-inch diameter

1 vine hops (*Humulus lupulus*), for approximately 70 sprigs, 6–8 inches long

floral scissors • fine-gauge gold wire • wire cutters

instructions under flap ➤

4 Cut the hops into approximately 70 sprigs, 6–8 inches long. Lay the first sprig along the ring and bind the stalk to it with gold wire.

5 Gradually build up the decoration by adding more sprigs of hops to the ring, overlapping them and binding them in place with gold wire as before, until the metal ring is completely hidden.

6 Finally, cut some short stems of hops and push the stalks directly into the arrangement, filling any gaps and concealing any visible wire.

1 Once complete, this candle arrangement will be difficult to move around, so either assemble it in situ or on a small tray or wooden board. Lay the metal ring flat on your surface and stand the four candles inside it, evenly spaced apart.

2 Cut the sisal rope into four lengths of 1½ yards. Wind one piece four times around one of the candles, roughly 3 inches from the base. Put one end of the rope though the metal ring and tie a secure double knot.

3 Use the three remaining lengths of rope to attach the ring to the other three candles in the same way, so the metal ring is suspended about 3 inches above the surface.

pumpkin display

On Halloween, hollowed-out pumpkins are seen everywhere, their crudely carved jack-o'-lantern faces illuminated by a candle placed inside. This tradition originated from the pagan belief that on the last night in October the souls of the dead revisited their homes; the garish faces carved into turnips and, later, pumpkins were thought to ward off evil spirits. For an alternative display, pumpkins make perfect natural containers for foliage, berries, and candles.

materials & equipment

pumpkin, approximately 7 inches high x 8½-inch diameter

1 block floral foam, 3 x 4½ x 3 inches

3 sprigs rosehips (*Rosa*)

5 sprigs blackberries (*Rubus fruticosus*)

5 sprigs guelder rose (*Viburnum opulus*)

8 sprigs fruiting ivy (*Hedera*)

3 purple beeswax candles, 10 inches long x 1¼-inch diameter

knife • spoon • medium-gauge wire • wire cutters

tape • floral scissors

instructions under flap ➤

5 Cut all the foliage into sprigs of approximately 6–8 inches. Arrange the rosehips around the candles, pushing the stems into the floral foam.

6 Add the sprigs of blackberries and guelder rose in the same way, spacing them evenly over the arrangement.

7 Finally, use the sprigs of fruiting ivy to fill in all the gaps between the other berries, making sure all the floral foam is concealed and that the display is a good shape with an even balance of color.

1 Using a sharp knife, cut out a neat square in the top of the pumpkin, measuring 3¼ x 3¼ inches. Lift off the top and then use a spoon to scoop out the flesh inside to a depth of about 4¾ inches.

2 Thoroughly soak the block of floral foam in water, then insert it snugly into the pumpkin, pushing it down so the top edge is flush with the surface of the pumpkin.

3 Cut six pieces of medium-gauge wire to approximately 4 inches long, and bend each one in half to form a hairpin shape. Tape two U-ends to the base of each of the three candles.

4 Place the three candles in a triangular formation in the block of floral foam, anchoring them in place with the wires.

tree of ivy

This is a great alternative to a traditional Christmas tree and can be redecorated time and again. The cone is carved out of blocks of floral foam and covered with chicken wire through which tendrils of ivy are woven. I love the Victorian idea of hanging candles on a tree, but have never felt happy using holders that clip onto branches. These candles are held securely in place with lengths of wire spiraled around the base of each and pushed into the cone.

materials & equipment

terracotta flowerpot, approximately 8 inches high x 10-inch diameter

dry-hard clay or quick-drying cement

$\frac{1}{2}$-inch wooden stick, approximately 32 inches long

enough floral foam to make a cone approximately 26 inches high,
20 inches in diameter at widest point, narrowing to about 1$\frac{1}{4}$ inches at the top;
you will need 2$\frac{1}{2}$ blocks floral foam, 21$\frac{1}{2}$ x 12$\frac{1}{2}$ x 9 inches

2-inch chicken wire, 26 x 60 inches

19 candles, 6 inches long x 1$\frac{1}{2}$-inch diameter

9 yards heavy-gauge wire

approximately 150 strands trailing ivy (*Hedera*), 14–28 inches long

30 yards red wire-edged ribbon with gold trimming, 2 inches wide

knife • glue • wire cutters • tape • needle • thread

instructions under flap ➤

7 Make 20 ribbon roses to decorate the tree. For each rose, cut a 1½-yard length of wire-edged ribbon. Grasp one of the wire ends and gather the ribbon along that edge until it measures approximately 30 inches. Make an overhand knot in the wire to prevent the gathers from slipping out. Grasp the bottom corner of ribbon where the wire protrudes and fold the top corner over to the bottom edge to make a triangle.

8 Holding the top of the triangle, fold the base in half and squeeze it together to make the center of the rose. Still holding the base of the triangle tightly with one hand, wind the long end of wire several times around it to form the "stem."

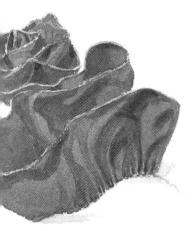

9 Wrap the ribbon around the stem a few times, keeping the gathered bottom edges flush. Then wind the end of the wire around the stem to hold the folds in place.

10 Fold the ribbon back on itself in the opposite direction and then back again to make a tuck. Secure the folds with the wire as before.

11 Continue wrapping the gathered ribbon around the stem to fill out the rose, securing the folds with the wire as you go. After every few folds, make a tuck in the ribbon as before (*see* step 10) and secure it with the wire.

12 When the rose is finished, wind the wire end securely around the stem, leaving the loose end to attach the rose to the tree. Finally, make a few stitches in the stem of the rose with matching thread to prevent it from unraveling.

13 Make another 19 roses in the same way and attach them evenly around the tree, tying them onto the chicken wire with the loose ends of wire.

1 Fill the flowerpot with dry-hard clay or cement, then push the stick vertically into the center of the pot and and leave it to set.

2 Cut and glue the blocks of floral foam together to form a stack 26 inches high. Then, when the glue has dried, use a sharp knife to carve it into a cone shape.

3 Push the cone centrally onto the stick until its base rests on the rim of the pot. Wrap chicken wire around the cone, trim off the excess, and twist the edges together to hold it in place.

4 Cut two pieces of wire 8 inches long and bend them into hairpin shapes. Tape them to the base of one of the candles. Then cut 18 pieces of wire 18 inches long and wrap a piece twice around the base of each candle, bringing the ends parallel to each other so they protrude horizontally by about 4 inches.

5 Push the first candle into the top of the cone. Then, starting near the top of the tree, push the other candles into the floral foam in three rows of four, six, and eight; the horizontal wires will anchor the candles in the floral foam.

6 Cut a selection of long and short lengths of ivy and weave them vertically through the chicken wire until the cone and wire are completely covered. Tuck in or trim off any stray ends.

gilded ring

Willow branches, which are flexible enough to bend, were used to fashion the circular ring onto which four legs were glued to make the basic structure for this festive candle decoration. The frame was sprayed gold, together with a collection of tiny pine cones, poppy seedheads, and oak leaves, which were then bound onto the ring with fine gold wire. Not only does it look stunning on a side table, this gilded ring also makes an unusual table centerpiece.

materials & equipment

for a ring approximately 12 inches in diameter:

5 branches willow (*Salix*), approximately 16 inches long x ½-inch diameter

8 sturdy sticks, 4 inches long x ¼-inch diameter

32 small pine cones

at least 64 sprigs oak leaves (*Quercus*), approximately 3 inches long

16 poppy seedheads (*Papaver*)

4 gold candle holders

4 gold candles, 10 inches long x ½-inch diameter

spool wire • wire cutters • glue • coarse sandpaper

scrap paper • gold spray paint • gold wire

instructions under flap ➤

6 Form a cluster of three pine cones by winding a length of gold wire around the base of each cone in between the lower scales. Twist the ends together, then wrap the wires securely around the ring.

7 Group the remaining pine cones in clusters of fives and threes and wire them onto the ring in alternating groups on each side of the candle holders.

8 Use the gold wire to bind the oak leaves together in clusters and then wire them onto the ring, placing some around the candle holders and others between the groups of pine cones.

9 Complete the decoration by slotting four poppy seedheads among each of the central clusters of oak leaves in between the groups of pine cones. Finally, place the candles in the holders.

1 To make them easier to bend into a circle, flex all the willow branches a few times before you begin. Then take the first two pieces and hold them together so they overlap each other by roughly half their length. Bind the ends together with spool wire.

2 Build up the circle, overlapping each branch by roughly half its length and binding the ends tightly together with wire to make a sturdy, double-thickness ring.

3 Pair up the eight sturdy sticks and glue them at regular intervals to the inside edge of the ring to form four legs. Reinforce them by binding them securely to the ring with wire. Check that the ring will stand without wobbling, and, if necessary, level the feet with sandpaper.

4 Place the finished ring and all the leaves, pine cones, and poppy seedheads on scrap paper and spray them thoroughly with gold paint. Leave until completely dry.

5 Glue the four candle holders securely in place on the ring, positioning them directly above the four legs.

candles galore

There is a magnificent variety of candles on the market, from the simplest rolled candles, made from sheets of natural beeswax wrapped around a wick, to the basic, traditional dipped candles, formed by dipping the wick, often in pairs, into melted wax. Until the discovery of paraffin wax in the 1850s, these dipped candles were made from natural wax—either tallow, derived from mutton fat, or, the most romantic and most coveted, beeswax—dipped layer by layer until the required size had been achieved, a process that has remained unchanged for the last 500 years.

Essentially, candlemaking can be regarded as a kind of art, since it is the creation of a sculptured form. Wax is one of the oldest modeling materials, and amazing waxen images have been recovered from the pyramids. There is evidence of a 15th-century Parisian who experimented by using wooden molds to make candles, and he was soon imitated by others. Nowadays, some of the most popular candles are those cast from molten wax into every shape imaginable, using molds of metal, plastic, and rubber, providing a huge variety of candles in a broad spectrum of sizes.

Candles were originally the primary source of light and, consequently, they were designed to be burned for several hours at a time. Now that most are used for purely esthetic reasons, many of the large candles are not lit for long enough to produce a good pool of wax to burn evenly. Pressing the outer edges of the candle toward the flame will help, but if too much wax melts, it may cause the flame to smoke and will eventually drown it. Another helpful tip is to wrap candles in foil and place them in the refrigerator for several hours before they are lit: this will make them burn much more evenly and slowly. To prevent candles from dripping excessively, try to place them out of direct drafts and make sure they are set vertically, whether in candle holders or floral foam bases, and placed on a flat surface.

The best way to clean a candle is to rub the surface with an abrasive fabric, such as nylon or chiffon, which will remove dust and dirt. Alternatively, scrape a knife blade lightly against the wax and then polish it with mineral spirits. Another way to restore shine is to polish the candle with a drop of olive oil on a soft cloth.

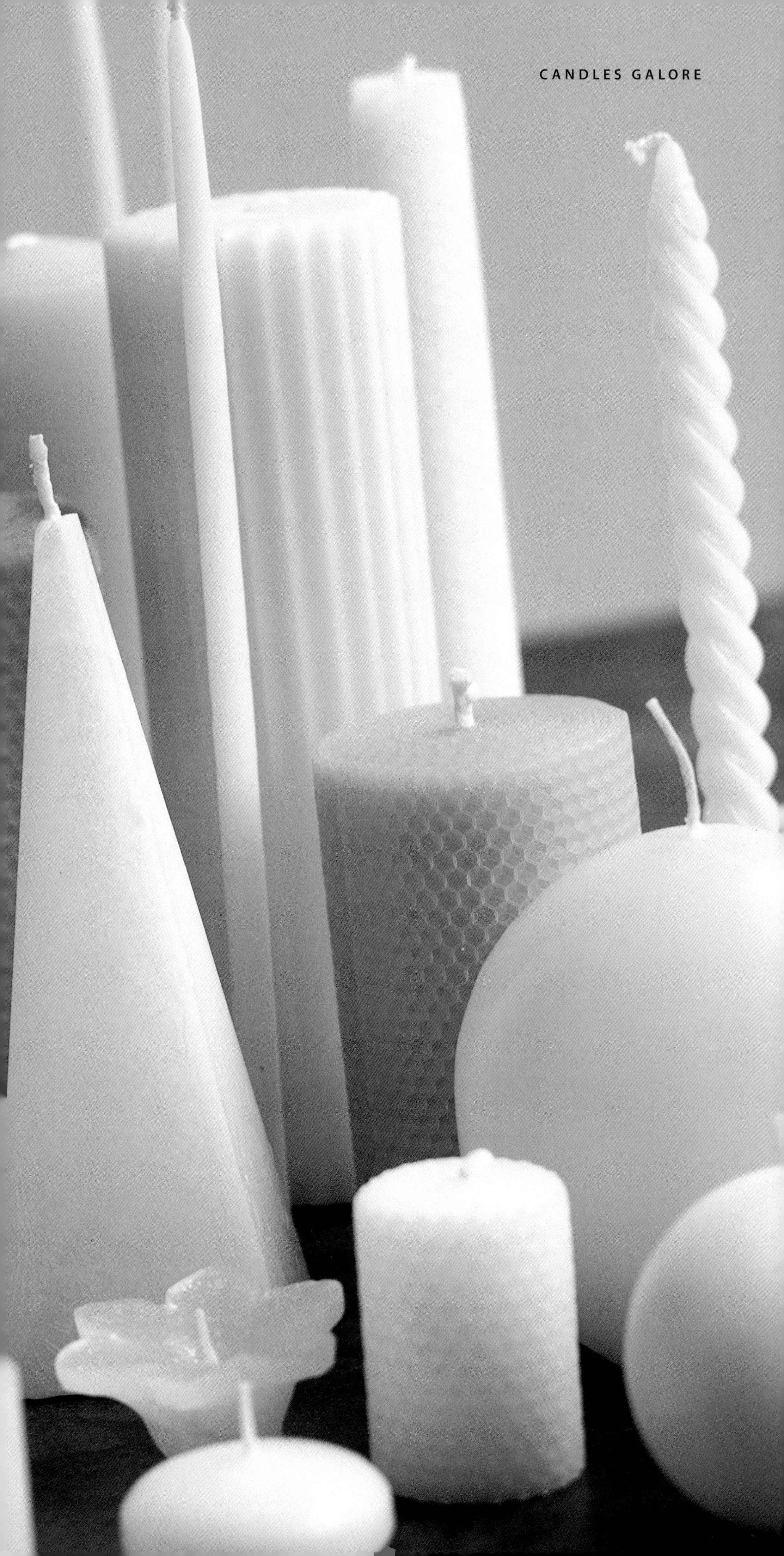

CANDLES GALORE

Whatever the shape and size of the candle, the wick will generally be made of braided cotton and should be trimmed to about 1/2 inch—if it is longer than 1 inch, the flame will smoke. However, if the wick is too short, the flame will drown in the well of molten wax. A small wick may also cause the candle to drip excessively, since the flame will melt the wax faster than it can be burned and the excess will spill over the sides. To lengthen the wick, use a match to melt the wax around its base and pour some away.

Color adds to the sensual pleasure of candles, and with all the colors of the rainbow available, from the subtlest pastels to the most vibrant primary hues, it should be easy to find a shade to complement the

color scheme of your room and the design of the decoration you are making. You can either choose bold contrasting colors to create a dramatic visual statement, or select tones that link up with the color scheme of the room or table linen for a more under-stated and elegant look. Colored liquid oil, which is burned directly into the atmosphere, is a clean alter-native to candles and looks stylish in glass burners.

Scent can have a powerful effect on mood, and all sorts of aromatic candles are available for every occasion, whether you wish to use a stimulating scent to create a special ambience for a dinner party or important event, or a calming or uplifting fragrance to create a relaxing or sensual atmosphere in the

home. Also, citronella candles are ideal for burning outside, since their sharp lemony scent deters insects. Beeswax candles are naturally perfumed with a wonderful sweet fragrance, but there are many different ways candles can be enhanced artificially, with scented material or oils incorporated into the wax, or by surrounding candles with decorative displays of highly fragranced herbs, flowers, or fruit. Some candles are made with synthetically produced oils, and they are the most versatile and inexpensive. My favorite fragrances are natural, unadulterated perfumes derived from plants. However, since a great number of flowers are required to make just a small quantity of many of the essential oils, aromatherapy candles are relatively expensive.

Instead of requiring traditional holders, many candles come complete with their own containers—from simple tea lights, which can be floated on a little water in small glass holders, to larger glass jars, rustic terracotta or contemporary painted flowerpots, galvanized metal buckets, tin cans, or seashells. Many are specially designed for outdoor use and have wider wicks to enable them to withstand a breeze. The smaller containers look lovely grouped together in clusters on a table or wall, while larger ones, placed around the perimeters of a terrace or lawn, bathe the yard in a soft flickering glow; as the wax burns, the rim of the container protects the flame from breezes. Torches, wedged into a container or anchored in the earth, also create wonderful lighting effects outside.

materials, equipment, & techniques

candle holders & containers

Fat pillar candles are able to stand unsupported on a flat surface, although they should be placed on a mat or plate to protect the surface from dripping wax. There are innumerable options for smaller candles, aside from the vast selection of candlesticks and candelabras available. For example, simple terracotta flowerpots make attractive containers, decorated with a little moss and filled with a nonflammable substance like sand or gravel. The choice of container or holder for the candle or candles is integral to the overall look of the decoration, and with a practically unlimited number of bowls, glasses, flowerpots, candlesticks, and candelabras in every conceivable style, the scope for creativity is endless. Whether you aim for a simple understated look—using an ordinary glass votive holder, a standard plastic bowl or tray, or a basic flowerpot—or whether you opt for an elaborate, decorative candelabra on which to focus your design, the candle or candles should never overpower the container and look top-heavy. All kinds of natural raw materials—flowers, foliage, shells, pine cones, fruits, and vegetables—look great alongside candles, and many small fruits or vegetables can be hollowed out to make fun candle holders—melons, squashes, cabbages, artichokes, and pumpkins: let your imagination run riot.

supports

One of the most valuable supports for anchoring wired objects is moss, which comes in many different forms, both fresh and dried, and is also valued for its decorative qualities. In 1954 Smithers-Oasis invented floral foam, which is so essential to many of the arrangements in this book, but it did not become widely available and affordable until the 1970s, before which time moss was the basis of most flower arrangements. Floral foam is ideal for incorporating candles into a decoration and provides great design versatility. In addition to the standard brick, available in several sizes, different shaped blocks and wreath frames can also be purchased. Alternatively, it is simple to create your own designs by gluing standard bricks together and carving them into shapes. Green floral foam is designed to soak up water to prolong the life of fresh flowers and can only be used once. It should be placed in water and allowed to sink naturally, at which point it is fully saturated. To prevent flowers from fading, keep the floral foam moist by adding water as necessary. Brown floral foam, which is much harder in texture, is for use with dried flowers and other nonliving materials.

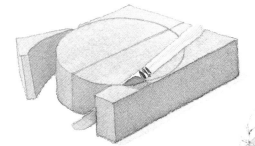

Standard floral foam bricks can be glued together to create larger blocks, which can then be carved into any shape (above and right); a floral foam wreath frame makes a useful surround for a home-made cone (right); while an ordinary candlestick can be adapted to hold flowers as well as a candle by taping a block of floral foam to the holder (far right).

Candles can be grouped for visual impact by taping their bases together, incorporating wooden sticks to anchor them in place.

Use two or more pieces of medium- or heavy-gauge wire to wire a candle, depending on its size. Bend the wires into hairpin shapes and tape the U-ends around the base.

anchoring candles

Many florists sell special holders for standard candles, which have pointed bases that can be pushed into floral foam. Alternatively, any size candle can be anchored into floral foam using either wire or wooden sticks. Medium-gauge wire, cocktail sticks, or toothpicks are ideal for standard candles, while larger pillar candles require stronger supports, such as heavy-gauge wire, wooden skewers, or garden stakes. To use wire, depending on the size of the candle, cut two or more lengths between 4 and 8 inches and bend them into U-shapes. Hold one bent end on each side of the candle between 1 1/4 and 2 1/2 inches from the base, then tape them in place, using waterproof floral tape if the candle is to be placed in wet floral foam. Alternatively, tape three or more wooden sticks vertically around the base of the candle. The protruding ends of the wires or sticks can then be inserted into the floral foam, or even into chicken wire crumpled up in the base of a vase. If a candle holder does not have a pricket, candles can be held securely in place using a small ball of florist's removable adhesive—a waterproof claylike substance. For tabletop displays, avoid placing candles at eye-level and try to vary the height of the flowers and candles to avoid monotony.

Instead of wire, wooden sticks, such as skewers or garden stakes, can be taped at regular intervals around the base of a candle. The protruding sticks can then be pushed into the floral foam to hold the candle in place. The number of sticks you use and how long they are will depend on the size of your chosen candle.

conditioning flowers

Prepare all stems on a sheet of plastic to protect the surface and make cleaning up easier. A sharp knife and sturdy floral scissors are essential, and shears are useful for cutting tough woody stems. If you gather flowers from the yard, wait for a cool day when the flowers are less likely to fade and take a bucket of water in which to place the cut stems. When flowers are left out of water, the stems will begin to dry out, preventing them from taking up water, so always cut at least 1 inch off the ends, trimming away snags, thorns, and any foliage that will be underwater. All flowers should be cut cleanly on the diagonal to create maximum surface area for water to be taken up while causing minimum damage to the stem cells. Stems should always be cut above, rather than directly below, hard nodules to facilitate drinking.

There are many ways to revive wilting flowers: roses can be wrapped in paper to protect the heads from steam and the stem ends plunged into boiling water for a few minutes; tulips can be tightly wrapped in paper and left for several hours in a bucket of water directly under a light in a cool room to prevent the stems from bending, while delicate blooms, such as violets, can be revived by submerging the flowers in water for up to an hour. Running cool water over the stems and spraying flower heads with a misting spray also helps prevent wilting. The temperature of the water also influences its uptake, and lukewarm water is ideal, since it has less oxygen than cold water, which allows it to travel up the stems more easily.

Before arranging flowers, let them drink a mixture of fresh, lukewarm water and flower food in a container that has been scrupulously cleaned with a few drops of bleach. Leave them soaking for a few hours to revive them and allow the stems to firm up; this is especially important for sappy stems, which may otherwise contaminate the water. Let the flowers stand in the water until they are needed. Flower food, which can also be mixed with the water used to soak floral foam, prolongs the life of flowers by providing them with nourishment and releasing an antibacterial agent. All flowers should be kept away from direct sunlight, heat, and drafts and, whether they are arranged in vases or floral foam, they should be refreshed frequently by topping them up with water and flower food, changing the water, and spraying them using a misting spray. Any dead heads or leaves should be removed immediately, since they emit ethylene, which causes flowers to age.

The only flowers that require special treatment are daffodils (*Narcissi*) and poppies (*Papaver*). There are special flower foods for the narcissus family, which emit a slime that may be harmful to other flowers. These should be left to soak in a bucket of water with a few drops of bleach for some time before arranging them with other flowers. Poppies exude a milky latex when cut, so usually the grower will singe the cut ends to prevent the flowers from flagging. If you recut the stems, singe the ends over a match or candle flame.

wiring, tying, & bonding

Wires are used to support and control flower stems and also to make arrangements more stable. The question of which wire to use is a difficult one and only practice will be able to guide you. Although there are certain rules about which kind of wire to use for which flower, no two stems are identical: for example, winter roses forced under artificial light have much weaker stems than those grown in the summer in natural conditions. Most wires, available from florists, garden centers, and hardware stores, are defined by their diameter and length, either in the traditional standard wire gauge or in metric measurements. Therefore, a medium wire of medium length would

be 0.027 x 7 inches or 0.7 x 180 mm. Some wires are annealed, which gives them a blue tinge, and some are covered by a green coating that prevents them from rusting. This is also useful, since it camouflages the wire when it is incorporated into a flower arrangement. Very fine wire is suitable for wiring the most delicate flowers, as well as individual flowerets and leaves. Medium-gauge wire is useful for supporting most flowers and for wiring sprigs of foliage into small bunches. Heavy-gauge wire should be used for large flowers and any heavy fruit or vegetable, which need a stronger support. As a general rule, floral wires should be used to reinforce stems or to make false stems, while spool wire should be used for any binding job, such as sculpting moss into a shape or securing foliage onto a base. Where material is grouped for visual impact, floral wire can be used to bind stems together before incorporating them into arrangements. Lengths of wire can also be bent into U-shapes and used to pin moss, twigs, or leaves onto a base of floral foam.

String, raffia, and rope are useful and decorative, and a selection of tapes, especially waterproof floral tape, which can be used to secure wet floral foam, seal stem ends, and conceal wire, is fundamental. Strong glue is also essential, and a hot glue gun is a good addition to any craft kit, as it is a great time-saver and can stick wet material; but it should be used with care. Florist's removable claylike adhesive, which sticks to damp surfaces, is useful for securing pin holders to dishes, and candles or candle cups into holders or vases.

To wire a leaf, thread a piece of fine-gauge wire through the large main vein at the back of the leaf. Then bring the two ends together and twist them around the stem of the leaf to make a double-leg mount.

Most fruit and vegetables can be wired using the following method. Push a 10-inch length of heavy-gauge wire through the bottom one-third of the fruit. Bring the ends around the base of the fruit and twist them tightly together.

Use medium-gauge wire to reinforce stems or to make bunches. Bend the wire into a hairpin shape, with one leg longer than the other. Hold the U-end against the stem or stems and wind the long leg around the stem and the other leg of wire.

plant directory

Alchemilla mollis (**lady's mantle**)
pp. 12, 66
Yellow-green feathery flowers with
softly rounded green leaves.
CARE Cut stem ends cleanly at an angle
underwater, then condition and leave
them soaking in deep water.

Anethum graveolens (**dill**) p. 70
Aromatic foliage with delicate frondy
leaves.
CARE Cut stem ends cleanly at an angle,
then condition and soak in water.

Arundinaria (**bamboo**) p. 16
Stout rigid canes, which are decorative
and can also be used to add support
to arrangements.
CARE Keep dry and away from direct
sunlight.

Asparagus densiflorus (**asparagus fern**)
pp. 66, 70
A foliage plant with delicate feathery
leaves.
CARE Cut stem ends cleanly at an angle,
then condition and soak in water. Mist the
leaves to prevent them from drying out.

Aspidistra (**aspidistra**) p. 16
Long-lasting, leathery, glossy leaves,
which are lance-shaped tapering to a
pointed tip; may be variegated.
CARE Cut stem ends cleanly at an angle,
then condition and soak in water.

Betula (**birch**) p. 74
Mid- to dark green foliage and
attractive ornamental stems.
CARE Cut stem ends cleanly at an angle,
then feed with food for woody-
stemmed plants and soak in water.

Brassica (**ornamental cabbage**) p. 42
Available in varying sizes, some with
variegated pink, white, or green
foliage; sold as a cut flower on a long
stem when it has gone to seed.
CARE Cut stem ends cleanly at an angle,
then condition and soak in water. Change
vase water frequently to prevent it from
creating an unpleasant odor.

Buxus (**boxwood**) pp. 12, 56, 66
A dense, slow-growing, evergreen tree
or shrub with small, shiny leaves.
CARE Cut stem ends cleanly at an angle,
then condition and soak in water.

Celosia argentea (**cockscomb**) pp. 38, 70
Vibrant crests of deep red, orange,
crimson, or yellow flowers.
CARE Cut stem ends cleanly at an angle,
then condition and soak in water.

Cinnamomum camphora (**cinnamon**)
p. 16
Spice used for culinary purposes. The
brown sticks can be purchased from
dried-flower and herbal suppliers.
CARE Store in a dark, dry place.

Citrus aurantiifolia (**lime**) pp. 56, 60
Green, oval, edible fruits produced by a
small Asian tree with stiff, sharp spines.
CARE Store in a cool, dark, damp place.

Citrus limon (**lemon**) p. 60
Yellow, oval, edible fruits produced
by a small Asian evergreen tree.
CARE Store in a cool, dark, damp place.

Citrus unshiu (**satsuma**) p. 60
Edible fruits with loose orange rind
and easily separable segments,
produced by a small citrus tree.
CARE Store in a cool, dark, damp place.

Cotinus (**smoke bush**) p. 42
Leaves are disk-shaped and purple.
CARE Cut stem ends and plunge them
into boiling water; add cold water until
tepid, then add flower food for woody-
stemmed plants and leave to soak.

Cucurbita (**pumpkin**) p. 88
Large round fruit with thick orange
rind and pulpy flesh, produced by a
creeping plant.
CARE Store in a cool, damp environment
to prevent the skin from drying out.

Cynara cardunculus (**cardoon**) p. 24
Large thistlelike plant with spiny
leaves and spherical purple flowers.
CARE Strip away foliage to maintain
flower heads; cut stems cleanly at an
angle, then condition and soak in water.

Cynara Scolymus Group (**globe
artichoke**) p. 16
Thistlelike plant, which produces large,
edible flower heads containing many
fleshy scalelike bracts.
CARE Store in a cool, dark, damp place
and, when used in decorations, keep
away from direct heat to prolong life.

Dasylirion (**bear grass**) p. 16
Long, thin strands of strong dark
green grass.
CARE Cut stem ends cleanly at an angle,
then condition and soak in water.

Equisetum (**snake grass**) p. 16
Long green reeds with beige rings at
irregular intervals.
CARE Cut and place in water or store
wrapped in wet paper.

Euphorbia myrsinites (**spurge**)
pp. 66, 70, 78
Evergreen perennial with spirally
arranged blue-gray leaves, with long-
lasting yellow-green flowers.
CARE Cut stem ends cleanly at an angle
and plunge them into boiling water;
add cold water until tepid, then add
flower food and leave to soak.

Eustoma grandiflorum (**lisianthus**) p. 78
Delicate bell-shaped flowers, either
individual blooms or in panicles, in
shades of white, purple, blue, and pink.
CARE Cut stem ends cleanly at an angle,
then condition and soak in water.

Fritillaria pinardii (**fritillary**) p. 74
Bell-shaped red-orange flowers with
yellow-tipped petals suspended from
slender stems.
CARE Cut stem ends cleanly at an angle,
then condition and place in deep water
for a few hours before arranging.

Galax (**galax**) pp. 12, 38
Heart-shaped, shiny, leathery leaves,
which turn a dark red-bronze in fall
and are long lasting when cut.
CARE Cut stem ends cleanly at an angle,
then condition and soak in water.
Alternatively, preserve the leaves by
wrapping them in damp paper.

Gloriosa (**glory lily**) p. 70
Red or yellow lilylike flowers with
attractive wavy margins.
CARE Cut stem ends cleanly at an angle,
then condition and soak in water.

Hebe (**hebe**) pp. 12, 56, 66
Attractive foliage plant, which
produces flower clusters in mauve,
pink, or white.
CARE Cut stem ends cleanly at an angle,
then condition and soak in water.

Hedera (**ivy**) pp. 42, 46, 52, 60, 66, 70, 88, 92
Lobe-shaped leaves in a wide range of sizes in solid green or variegated.
CARE Cut stem ends cleanly at an angle, then condition and soak in water.

Humulus lupulus (**hop**) p. 84
A climbing plant with green conelike female flowers and clusters of small male flowers.
CARE Store in damp paper with stem ends in water.

Hydrangea (**hydrangea**) p. 78
Very large long-lasting pink, blue, or white flower heads.
CARE Cut stem ends cleanly at an angle, then condition and soak in water; leave flower heads submerged in cool water for a few hours before arranging.

Iris (**flag iris**) p. 78
White, yellow, brown, lilac, and, most commonly, blue flowers, with long, swordlike leaves.
CARE Cut stem ends cleanly at an angle, then condition and soak in water.

Laurus nobilis (**laurel**) p. 16
Glossy, dark green, oval leaves up to 6 inches long.
CARE Cut stem ends cleanly at an angle, then condition and soak in water.

Leucospermum cordifolium (**pincushion protea**) p. 12
Large spherical flowers with numerous forward-arching styles, usually orange, but also crimson or yellow.
CARE These are hardy flowers. Cut stem ends cleanly at an angle, then condition and soak in water.

Magnolia (**magnolia**) p. 16
Leaves are green and glossy, and flowers are large and usually fragrant, available in many different shapes, in white, purple, pink, yellow, or green.
CARE Cut stem ends cleanly at an angle, then condition and soak in water.

Mentha (**mint**) p. 42
Aromatic plant used mainly for culinary purposes, available in many varieties; the variegated varieties have particularly attractive leaves.
CARE Cut stem ends cleanly at an angle and remove lower foliage, then condition and soak in deep water.

Narcissus papyraceus (**paper white**) p. 52
Elegant trumpet-shaped white flowers with a heady scent.
CARE Cut stem ends cleanly at an angle, then condition and leave in water overnight to allow excess sap to drain away.

Origanum (**marjoram**) p. 38
Pretty, delicate, aromatic, purplish-red herb, used mainly for culinary purposes, but also ideal for use in decorative scented arrangements.
CARE Cut stem ends cleanly at an angle, then condition and soak in water.

Papaver (**poppy**) pp. 66, 96
The short-lived flowers are wide-spreading, bowl-, cup-, or saucer-shaped in an array of colors. Buds are followed by distinctive "pepper-pot" seedpods.
CARE Singe stem ends over the flame of a candle or match to seal the sap in. Then condition and place in deep water.

Photinia (**photinia**) pp. 12, 42
Bright red young foliage, with leaves that are alternate, lance-shaped to broadly ovate.
CARE Try to avoid cutting when new growth is very young. Cut stem ends cleanly at an angle, then condition and soak in water.

Pittosporum (**pittosporum**) p. 42
Lustrous and long-lasting evergreen foliage with small ovate leaves; some varieties are variegated. Attractive, useful foliage for flower arrangements.
CARE Cut stem ends cleanly at an angle, then condition and soak in water.

Polygonatum (**Solomon's seal**) pp. 66, 78
Arched stems with hanging flowers, which are waxy in appearance and greenish white in color.
CARE Cut stem ends cleanly at an angle, then condition and place in tepid water for a few hours before using.

Prunus (**cherry blossom**) pp. 74, 78
Elegant branches with sprays of white, pink, or red flowers in spring.
CARE Cut stem ends cleanly at an angle, then feed with food for woody-stemmed plants and soak in water.

Quercus (**oak**) pp. 42, 96
Glossy, dark green leaves, which are oblong-obovate with irregular lobes.
CARE Cut stem ends cleanly at an angle, then feed with food for woody-stemmed plants and soak in water.

Rosa (**rosehip**) pp. 42, 88
Bright orange, oval, berrylike fruit on brown woody stems.
CARE Cut stem ends cleanly at an angle and remove any unwanted foliage, then feed with food for woody-stemmed plants and soak in water.

Rosa 'Anna' (**rose**) p. 70
Pink "raspberry-ripple" rose, the petals of which have a vanilla tone with dark pink edges.
CARE Cut stem ends cleanly at an angle, then condition and soak in water.

Rosa 'Delilah' (**rose**) p. 52
New variety of lilac rose that opens beautifully and is long lasting.
CARE Cut stem ends cleanly at an angle, then condition and soak in water.

Rosa 'Jacaranda' (**rose**) p. 52
Bright pink rose with a strong fragrance.
CARE Cut stem ends cleanly at an angle, then condition and soak in water.

Rosa 'Macarena' (**rose**) p. 70
New variety of strong peach-colored rose, which is a spray rose and is popular as it looks like a garden rose.
CARE Cut stem ends cleanly at an angle, then condition and soak in water.

Rosa 'Miracle' (**rose**) p. 12
Bright orange standard rose, which opens well and lasts a long time.
CARE Cut stem ends cleanly at an angle, then condition and soak in water.

Rosa 'Ravel' (**rose**) p. 70
Large-headed, bright pink rose, which lasts well.
CARE Cut stem ends cleanly at an angle, then condition and soak in water.

Rosmarinus officinalis (**rosemary**) p. 52
Spiny, strongly aromatic leaves, with small mauve-white flowers. Generally used as a culinary herb.
CARE Cut stem ends cleanly at an angle, then condition and soak in water. Remove all lower leaves to keep water clean and free from bacteria.

Rubus fruticosus (**blackberry**) p. 88
A woody plant with thorny stems and edible fruits, which are black or dark purple and glossy.
CARE Cut stem ends cleanly at an angle, then feed with food for woody-stemmed plants and soak in water.

Salix (**willow**) p. 96
Flexible branches with attractive bark, catkins, and leaves.
CARE Cut stem ends, then feed with food for woody-stemmed plants and place in deep water.

Senecio cineraria (**dusty miller**) p. 78
Silver-gray felted leaves with yellow daisylike flowers.
CARE Cut stem ends cleanly at an angle, then condition and soak in water.

Spiraea (**spirea**) p. 70
Thin woody branches with tiny, white flower clusters.
CARE Cut stem ends cleanly at an angle, then feed with food for woody-stemmed plants and soak in water.

Stephanotis floribunda (**stephanotis**) p. 56
Strongly fragrant, delicate, star-shaped, waxy, white flowers, with dark green, shiny foliage.
CARE Cut stem ends or flowerets cleanly at an angle and place in a shallow bowl of water.

Syringa (**lilac**) p. 78
Woody tree, which in spring bears scented blossom of tiny flowerets in white, blue, mauve, and lilac.
CARE Cut stem ends cleanly at an angle, then feed with food for woody-stemmed plants and soak in water.

Viburnum opulus (**guelder rose**) pp. 42, 70, 88
Lobed, deep green leaves, with fragrant white flowers and clusters of red berries.
CARE Cut stem ends cleanly at an angle, then feed with food for woody-stemmed plants and soak in water.

Viola odorata (**violet**) p. 12
Sweetly fragrant flowers, most commonly rich purple in color, but also available in pink and white; the petals have a velvety texture.
CARE Cut stem ends cleanly at an angle, then submerge flowers in cool water and leave them to soak for a few hours.

Vitis vinifera (**grape**) p. 34
Edible fruit of the grapevine, which is purple or green in color.
CARE Store in a cool, dark, damp place.

Zantedeschia (**calla lily**) p. 52
Trumpet-shaped flowers with a large yellow spadix, most commonly available in white.
CARE Cut stem ends cleanly at an angle and bind the ends with floral tape to prevent them from splitting, then place them in deep warm water overnight.

suppliers

Craft-store chains
You will be able to find most, if not all, of the supplies called for in this book at any comprehensive craft store near you. Listed below are the largest chains with stores around the country. Call the listed number or use your local Yellow Pages to locate a store in your area. If no instructions are included in the listing, an automated service will ask for your zip code and provide you with the nearest store.

Ben Franklin
There is no centralized number for this franchised chain; look in your local Yellow Pages for the nearest outlet.

Crafts and More
A Division of Ames Department Stores
800-746-7263

Fabri-Centers of America
216-656-2600; ask for Customer Service
This chain operates under different names in different regions of the country. Call, and they will locate the affiliate nearest you.

Frank's Nursery and Crafts
313-564-2507; ask for Customer Service

Garden Ridge
281-579-7901; ask for Customer Service

Hobby Lobby
405-745-1100; ask for Customer Service

MJ Designs, Inc.
972-304-2200; ask for Customer Service

Michaels Stores, Inc.
800-642-4235

A. C. Moore
609-228-6700

Old America Stores, L.P.
903-532-3000; ask the operator

Rag Shops, Inc.
973-423-1303; ask for Customer Service

Treasure Island
201-529-1771; press 2 for store locations

Wal-Mart
501-273-4000

Candles
Candles are widely available in all manner of stores, from supermarkets to gift shops. Listed below are some specialty and mail-order sources. Call for catalogs.

Carolina Candle Co.
P.O. Box 918
Elkin, NC 28621
336-835-6080
A nearly limitless collection of tapers, votives, tea lights, and pillars—scented and unscented—is available from this company. Various aromatherapy candles are also available.

Candlechem Company
32 Thayer Circle
P.O. Box 705
Randolph, MA 02368
781-963-4161; fax: 781-963-3440
Look here for products to make your own candles: basic and designer scents, dyes and pigments, wax additives, novelty, metal, and acrylic molds, waxes, beeswax sheets, equipment, and accessories.

Colonial Candles of Cape Cod
232 Main Street
Hyannis, MA 02601
Mail orders: 800-437-1238, ext. 24
Well-known manufacturer of pillars, hand-dipped tapers, and classic candles in a wide range of colors. If you can't find the color or length you are looking for, call the 800 number.

Covington Candle
976 Lexington Avenue
New York, NY 10021
212-472-1131
This shop offers tapers in 30 colors and six sizes, from / to 1 / inches, which will fit perfectly into different holders and decors. Pillars are also available in a number of sizes and to order.

Creative Candles
P.O. Box 412514
Kansas City, MO 64141
816-474-9711
Specializes in hand-dipped, state-of-the-art tapers, pillars, and spheres in 44 designer colors.

Eika Candles
225 Fifth Avenue
New York, NY 10010
212-448-1001
Germany's largest candlemaker brings old-world elegance in traditional designs as well as in scented candles. Also available are aromatherapy candles made from 100 percent beeswax or vegetable wax using natural essential oils.

Hanna's Potpourri Specialties, Inc.
1421 East 15th Street
Fayetteville, AR 72701-7217
800-327-9826
This company offers a complete line of aromatherapy products, including candles, oils, potpourri, and home fragrance accessories. They also sell scented candles.

Northern Lights Candles
3674 Andover Road
Wellsville, NY 14895
716-593-1200; fax: 716-593-6481
Candles of all varieties are available here, from scented to columns of geometric forms; also molded novelty and made-to-drip specialty candles.

Pourette Candle Making Supplies
1418 NW 53rd Street
P.O. Box 17056
Seattle, WA 98115
800-888-9425
They offer a complete selection of candlemaking supplies such as beeswax sheets, wax beads, block wax, molds, and wicks.

Wreaths & floral supplies
In addition to the mail-order and specialty sources listed below, see the listing of craft-store chains and check local craft and floral supply shops for wreath forms and floral foam, tools, accessories, and supplies. Purchase live flowers from local flower markets, greengrocers, and supermarkets for the freshest, least expensive, and most varied selection.

FloraCraft
One Longfellow Place
P.O. Box 400
Ludington, MI 49431
616-845-5127; fax: 616-845-0240

Distributors of wreath, topiary, and geometric forms made of Styrofoam™, extruded foam, and straw; also available is a vast array of floral supplies and accessories.

High Country Floral
P.O. Box 159
Carlton, WA 98814
800-372-2646; fax: 509-923-2037
Here you can find preserved and stem-dyed wreaths, garlands, and arches that look and feel fresh; also preserved and stem-dyed baby's breath in 18 colors as well as a wide selection of other preserved and dried flowers and leaves, herbs, and spices.

J & T Imports Dried Flowers
P.O. Box 642
Solana Beach, CA 92075
619-481-9781
Available here are all sorts of dried and preserved flowers and foliage, including rosebuds by the pound. While they sell mainly to retail shops, they will fill credit card orders of $50 or more.

Loose Ends
P.O. Box 20310
Keizer, OR 97307
503-390-7457
Here you'll find a wide selection of unusual natural-fiber papers, ribbons, and botanicals, including seagrass, raffia, dried fruits, and fungi.

Maple Ridge Supply
9528 South Bolton Road
Posen, MI 49776
888-881-1880
Metal wreath forms of all sizes and shapes are available from this company. They also make a simple new tool to close the prongs on the forms easily and evenly; its called the Quik-Crafter™.

May Silk
16202 Distribution Way
Cerritos, CA 90703
800-282-7455
A complete line of silk flowers, plants, foliage, trees, arrangements, and floral accessories is available here.

Nature's Holler
15739 Old Lowery Road North
Omaha, AR 72662
870-426-5489
Suppliers of grapevine wreaths, acorns, pods, pine cones, color-blushed wheat, dried assorted weeds and grasses, baby's breath, sunflowers, moss, bamboo, wood works—everything you could hope for to make dried arrangements.

Tom Thumb Workshops
14100 Lankford Highway
P.O. Box 357
Mappsville, VA 23407
800-526-6502
Dried and pressed flowers, skeletonized leaves, and craft products can be found here, along with potpourri, herbs, spices, and essential oils.

Ribbons, ties, & trimmings
Ribbons and decorative cording and other tie trims are widely available in craft, variety, fabric, and sewing notions stores. The sources listed below provide a selection of the more unusual.

Conso Products
P.O. Box 326
Union, SC 29379
800-845-2431
One of the largest distributors of decorative trims, cordings, ropings, tassels, and fringes in a variety of fibers.

Hollywood Trims
A division of the Prym-Dritz Corporation
P.O. Box 5028
Spartanburg, SC 29304
Manufacturers and distributors of rayon, cotton, and metallic trims, cordings, and tassels.

Lion Brand Ribbon
An affiliate of C.M. Offray & Son
Route 24
P.O. Box 601
Chester, NJ 07930
Well-known makers of craft and specialty ribbons of all sorts, including burlap. The ribbons, including wired kinds, come in a broad selection of colors, fabrics, and widths, and are widely available in craft and variety stores as well as floral supply shops.

M & J Trimming Co.
1008 Sixth Avenue
New York, NY 10018
212-391-9072
Has an outstanding collection of decorative trims, cording, ropings, tassels, and fringes in a variety of fibers.

M.P.R. Associates, Inc.
P.O. Box 7343
High Point, NC 27264
800-454-3331
This maker of nontraditional ribbons can provide you with paper lace, corrugated paper ribbons, wired and plain paper and metallic ribbons, paper raffia, and paper twist.

Maxwell • Wellington
811 West Evergreen, Suite 306
Chicago, IL 60622
312-943-2866; fax: 312-943-9194
Ribbons of paper, velvets, and metallics in a variety of widths are available with or without wires or as luscious handmade bows. Also available are ⅛-inch colored paper-covered wires to use for tendrils and stems.

Tinsel Trading Co.
47 West 38th Street
New York, NY 10018
212-730-1030
Offers a unique collection of vintage-to-contemporary trims, tassels, fringes, and cords.

Miscellaneous
Anthropologie
1801 Walnut Street
Philadelphia, PA 19103
215-564-2313
Good selection of garden accessories, with lots of interesting flowerpots. Nationwide locations; call for one nearby.

Colonial Williamsburg
Department 023
P.O. Box 3532
Williamsburg, VA 23187-3532
800-446-9240
Attractive glass hurricane lamps, candlesticks, and traditional garden accessories. Mail order. Catalog.

Crate & Barrel
P.O. Box 9059
Wheeling, IL 60090-9059
800-451-8217
A wonderful source of good-value china, glass and plastic containers. Nationwide locations; call for one near you. Mail order. Catalog.

Fiskars Manufacturing Corp.
7811 West Stewart Avenue
Wausau, WI 54401
715-842-2091
Manufacturers of fine-quality scissors, snippers, paper edgers and punchers, and the very useful all-purpose Craft-Snip, which can be used to cut a variety of heavy-duty materials. They also make excellent tools for gardening and floral work.

Gardener's Eden
P.O. Box 7307
San Francisco, CA 94120-7307
800-822-9600
Quality garden tools and accessories. Nationwide locations; call for one near you. Mail order. Catalog.

Home Depot
Has a wide selection of lumber, outdoor furniture, and plant material at discounted prices. Check your local telephone directory for your nearest store.

Pottery Barn
P.O. Box 7044
San Francisco, CA 94120-7044
800-588-6250
Moderately priced furnishings for indoors and out, including garden furniture, glassware, china, plastic, candlesticks, and hurricane lamps. Nationwide locations; call for one near you. For a catalog call 800-922-5507.

Smith and Hawken
2 Arbor Lane
P.O. Box 6900
Florence, KY 41022-6900
800-776-3336
A wide variety of plants, tools, ornaments, and furniture. Nationwide locations; call for one near you. Mail order. Catalog.

Walnut Hollow
Route 2
Dodgeville, WI 53533
800-395-5995
This company manufactures just about any unfinished wooden shape imaginable, from birdhouses to candle cups.

Wood-N-Crafts, Inc.
P.O. Box 140
Lakeview, MI 48850
800-444-8075
Fax: 517-352-6792
A good source for unfinished wood, such as candlesticks and candle cups, animals, miniatures, boxes, dowels, balls, buttons, beads, fruit, stars, and hearts.

U.S. Shell, Inc.
P.O. Box 1033
Port Isabel, TX 78578
956-943-1709; fax: 956-943-6901
Large supplier of packaged shells of all types, from common scallops to rare varieties.

acknowledgments

It has been a great pleasure to work on this book with such an accomplished photographer as James Merrell. James and I have been shooting three books simultaneously to capture all the seasons for each one, and I am so grateful to him for bringing his unique blend of good humor, calm intuition, and artistic talent to each day.

I am also grateful to the extremely artistic and imaginative stylists who have worked on this book, Nato Welton, Martin Bourne, and Margaret Caselton, who have all brought their own personal style to the project. I must also thank the talented illustrator, Lizzie Sanders, for her superb artworks.

Thank you to the long-suffering staff at Ryland Peters & Small for all their support in the making of this volume, especially Paul Tilby, Sally Powell, and Zia Mattocks. I am particularly grateful to Zia for ordering and making sense of my text, and for her diligent approach and gentle understanding when deadlines slipped!

I am extremely grateful to all my staff who contributed time and ideas to this book, and also to those who carried on the day-to-day business while I was away. Thanks especially to Ashleigh Hopkins, who continues to support me and hold together the business—not to mention her contribution to the company as a gifted and accomplished florist. I am also very grateful to Joan Cardoza for all her help with this book, for her calm and resourceful manner, and for her artistic input. Thank you to Anita Everard, who was called in to help us keep up with the immense speed of James's photography, and to add her talent and experience to some of the projects and topics. In recent years my school has become very popular in Japan, and I am extremely happy to have had the assistance on this project of Hiroko Odakura, Mikiko Tanabe, Fumiko Inoue, Tomoko Akamine, Shinako Atsumi, and Yoko Okasaki. They have all studied with me during the course of this book and have, in their own way, contributed many ideas and suggestions, and have painstakingly created some of the more intricate designs. Thank you also to my personal assistants during this project: Jane Houghton and Sophie Hindley.

Finally, I would personally like to thank: Flowers & Plants Association; all at New Covent Garden Flower Market; all at C Best; all at Candle Maker's Supplies; all at V V Rouleaux; all at Something Special; Gerhard Jenne at Konditor and Cook; Chris Johnson at Sia Parlane; Sybil Sylvester at Wildflower Designs; Ted Baker; Jim Brazier; Peter Lethbridge. Also, The Columbia Candle Works, which I stumbled upon by chance while passing through California, who gave me such a fabulous insight into candlemaking and whose enthusiasm fired me.

The publishers would like to thank Smithers-Oasis UK Ltd and R & R Saggers, Waterloo House, Newport, Essex.

credits

Pages 4 (*second from right*), 34, and 37
Green-and-white striped fabric: Ian Mankin.
Pages 8 and 16
Table and chairs: After Noah.
Page 10
Top right iron wall hanging: Avant Garden; *below top right* white wirework chandelier: The Source; *bottom left* cactus-shaped candle: Avant Garden; *bottom right* wickerwork box: Paperchase.

Page 32
Top left decorative candle: by Point à la Ligne, supplied by Michael Johnson Ceramics; *below top left* wooden table: David Wainwright; *center* glass dip dish: General Trading Company.
Page 33
Bottom left liter wine glass: Jerry's Home Store; floating flower candle: The Pier.
Page 37
Wine glasses, glass plates and bowls: The Pier.

Page 64
Top left flatware: Glazebrook and Co.; cups and saucers and yellow plates: The Source; *bottom left* colored fabric: The Source; purple candles: The Pier.
Page 65
Top left Ribbon roses: V V Rouleaux; plates and zinc chargers: Jerry's Home Store; placemats: The Pier; wooden table: David Wainwright.